Passing in the Works of
CHARLES W. CHESNUTT

Passing in the Works of
CHARLES W. CHESNUTT

Edited by Susan Prothro Wright
and Ernestine Pickens Glass

UNIVERSITY PRESS OF MISSISSIPPI
JACKSON

Margaret Walker Alexander Series in African American Studies

www.upress.state.ms.us

The University Press of Mississippi is a member of the
Association of American University Presses.

First printing 2010
∞
Library of Congress Cataloging-in-Publication Data

Passing in the works of Charles W. Chesnutt / edited by Susan Prothro Wright
and Ernestine Pickens Glass.
     p. cm. — (Margaret Walker Alexander series in African American studies)
   Includes bibliographical references and index.
   ISBN 978-1-60473-416-4 (cloth : alk. paper) 1. Chesnutt, Charles W. (Charles
     Waddell), 1858–1932—Criticism and interpretation. 2. Passing (Identity)—
Fiction. I. Wright, Susan Prothro. II. Glass, Ernestine Pickens.
   PS1292.C6Z8 2010
   813'.4—dc22   2009020701

British Library Cataloging-in-Publication Data available

To the memory of James Francis and Harriet Maxine Wright

For my husband, William Glass

Contents

Preface

Charles Chesnutt's writing is informed by a uniquely historical perspective, one that is often mistaken for what it is not—a subordination of "all things" African American to all things white. On the other hand, Chesnutt's imaginative historicizing is frequently dismissed as superficial when readers fail to recognize what it is—an often ironic or even harshly satiric attack on notions of white superiority balanced by an objective rendering of the human qualities, good and bad, of whites and all hues of African Americans. In sum, the richness of Chesnutt's writing requires a variety of critical approaches, and the essays in the collection rise to the challenge by looking at his works through a number of perspectives—intertextual, signifying/discourse analysis, narratological, formal, psychoanalytical, new historical, reader response, and performative, for example—all of which serve to recover the significance of Chesnutt's works in their on-going historical and literary contexts. The essays in this collection, grown out of special sessions on Chesnutt at Modern Language Association, American Literature Association, and College Language Association conferences, are included both because of their original approaches to Chesnutt's work and because of their illuminating intersection with each other, an exchange that serves to expand the understanding of Chesnutt's ideologies, his artistry, and his place in social and literary history while uncovering new paths of inquiry into Chesnutt scholarship.

In relation to the collection more specifically, the essays set out to illustrate Chesnutt's genius in transforming historical reality from an African American perspective into his writing without destroying his relationship with a white readership, both his target audience and the source of his livelihood. Related to the imaginative rendering of history in Chesnutt's works is the recurring theme of "passing," along with its various implications for American society. This concern provides the thread that ties together the essays in this collection. Performance in Chesnutt's fiction—whites passing for black, blacks passing for white, aristocrats posing as genteel, illiterate but astute slaves and former slaves posturing as ignorant and dependent in order to achieve autonomy, and, in general, appearance functioning as reality—produced a palatable "realism" for white readers. Indeed, as the essays in the collection will show, performance is part and parcel of all of the genres utilized by Chesnutt, including journal entries, speeches, and essays, as well as his short and long fiction.

Chesnutt's conjure tales, for example, steeped in the history of the ante- and postbellum South, are perfectly formulated to evidence the comfortable tension that existed between black and white people whose physical proximity belied their distinctly separate worlds. Not only do the tales humanize African Americans, but, less obviously, they also characterize Chesnutt's power to manipulate language and audience through a careful selection of subject into which Chesnutt introduces powerful performances of character through a seemingly ingenuous venue. In "Charles Chesnutt's Historical Imagination," the contouring first essay of the collection, Werner Sollors affirms this, pointing out that Chesnutt's use of magic in the frame tales is more modernist magic realism than fabulist invention, making the tales far more political than his contemporary audience would have recognized. Chesnutt's political motives—to effect full social, political, and legal enfranchisement for blacks—and his desire to convey them imaginatively as fictional works are made obvious from his earliest journal entries: his familiarity with the South and his knowledge and understanding of African Americans in their public and private lives, combined with his relationship with "the better class of white men in the south," would afford him the "ability [to] write a far better book about the South" than either Albion Tourgee or Harriett Beecher Stowe (*Journals*, March 16, 1880, 125–126).[1] His task is "twofold": African Americans are to "prepare . . . for social recognition and equality" through writing; in turn, the writing will lead whites "imperceptibly, unconsciously step by step to the desired state of feeling [full acceptance of blacks]" (*Journals*, May 29, 1880, 140). Reading the essays in this collection with Chesnutt's charge to himself in mind broadens and deepens the study of Chesnutt's work.

In response to the undertaking Chesnutt imposed on himself, he began testing his ability to reconstruct subtly the words and works of white European thinkers for his own political purposes early in his career. He did so very specifically in a speech he delivered to the black North Carolina Teachers Association in 1882. As SallyAnn Ferguson persuasively demonstrates in "Signifying the Other: Chesnutt's 'Methods of Teaching,'" in his speech, Chesnutt artfully elides, misquotes, and emends the texts of white thinkers, philosophers, and pedagogues to further his own aims to advance the educational opportunities for black students. Margaret Bauer's "On Flags and Fraternities: Lessons in History in Charles Chesnutt's 'Po' Sandy'" (1888), a thought-provoking intertextual study of one of Chesnutt's most powerful conjure stories, reinforces the notion of the conjure tales' ability to politicize, even today. Bauer writes about teaching "Po' Sandy" and the exigency of linking it historically and culturally from the antebellum South to modern America's continued romanticization of the Old South through symbols and practices. And the historical and literary significance of Chesnutt's short stories is no less powerful than that of the conjure tales. It is, after all, as Martha Cutter points out in "Passing as Narrative and Textual Strategy in Charles

Chesnutt's 'The Passing of Grandison'" (1898), Grandison's performance of the stereotypical Uncle Tom that allows him to triumph over slavery. In addition to the narratological implications of the story, Cutter proves that on a textual level performance in "Grandison"—and, by extension, other Chesnutt works—gained Chesnutt entrance into the parlors of mainstream white Americans, no insignificant feat for a turn-of-the-century African American author.

Chesnutt's novels are equally complex, both unequivocally rich and strikingly different from each other: they may be convincingly crafted as Romances or as realism, presented in part or whole as dream or vision, or studded with performances of passing on various levels. Illustrating the fecundity of Chesnutt's imagination, Aaron Ritzenberg, in "The Dream of History: Memory and the Unconscious in Charles Chesnutt's *The House behind the Cedars*" (1900), applies Freudian theory to *House* to uncover and explore the rupture between white reality and black "memory." Ritzenberg recognizes *House* itself as a textual performance of resistance that allows John Walden, the novel's mulatto protagonist, to blend into white postbellum society while retaining his bond with his African American roots. Susan Prothro Wright's "In the Wake of D. W. Griffith's *The Birth of a Nation:* Chesnutt's *Paul Marchand, F.M.C.* as Command Performance" highlights the historical backdrop of *Paul Marchand* (submitted for publication in 1921; 1999)[2] in relation to D. W. Griffith's explosive racist film *Birth* (1915) to illustrate the potential for Chesnutt's novel to challenge the wholly negative portrayal of blacks while subtly questioning the positive representation of whites. Wright draws attention to the apparent performances of race and caste along with other "filmic" qualities in *Paul Marchand* that would have checked the blatant stereotypes in *Birth*.

Dealing with problems of the color line later in the nineteenth and early twentieth centuries, Chesnutt's novels and short stories are permeated with the provocative and psychologically electrifying notion that through miscegenation white America created a continuing "civil war." Although miscegenation was systematically denied and, ironically, illegal, the result of the union between blacks and whites was obvious, and its negative effects could pit blood relatives against each other. The veiling effect of Chesnutt's fictionalization of miscegenation allowed readers to ignore the ocular proof of the practice while being forced to scrutinize closely the heartache and violence it perpetrated.

Chesnutt's portrayal of the ramifications of miscegenation is astutely addressed in the essays in the collection: three essayists' contributions intersect and expand upon each other's salient points in relation to Chesnutt's perception of essentialism, particularly in association with race but also with class, ethnicity, and/or sex. Keith Byerman examines *The House behind the Cedars* (1900) and *Paul Marchand, F.M.C.* through a historical lens in "Performing Race: Mixed-Race Characters in the Novels of Charles Chesnutt" to uncover Chesnutt's ironic suggestion, achieved through contrived plots and character portrayals, that whiteness rather than blackness is a "performance," irrationally based on the unstable markers of scientific theories, laws, and codes delineating whiteness at the turn of the nineteenth century. Donald Gibson, in "A Question of Passing or a Question of Conscience: Toward Resolving the Ending of *Mandy Oxendine*," responds to *Mandy Oxendine* (ca. 1897; 1997),[3] focusing on facets of language and narration that destabilize any patent designation of class and race. Gibson's reading offers a means of coming to terms with the indeterminacy of Mandy and Tom Landry's passing for white at the end of the novel. Scott Thomas Gibson, in "'They Were All Colored to the Life': Historicizing 'Whiteness' in *Evelyn's Husband*" (ca. 1900; 2005),[4] shows how Chesnutt clouds the binary white-black race issues of the turn of the century by including the ethnic-class concerns disquieting the United States at the same time. Gibson deconstructs concepts of race, class, and ethnicity to conclude that Chesnutt's appraisal of such notions remands them to the arena of on-going systematic racism.

While the collection is not a study that covers all of Chesnutt's works, the essays are in conversation with past and more recently published works on Chesnutt, including publications by several of the collection's contributors themselves. Two important recent monographs on Chesnutt, Matthew Wilson's *Whiteness in the Novels of Charles W. Chesnutt* (Jackson: UP of Mississippi, 2004) and Ryan Simmons's *Chesnutt and Realism: A Study of the Novels* (Tuscaloosa: U of Alabama P, 2006), are part of that conversation, implicitly and explicitly. Both works focus on Chesnutt's novels. In his book, Wilson includes seminal chapters on Chesnutt's "white-life" novels. Simmons, in his work, offers convincing evidence that Chesnutt *is* a literary realist in his own right. Although the essays in *Passing in the Works of Charles W. Chesnutt* interact with many other important critical works, many of which are acknowledged within the essays, I feel it is important to mention here Dean McWilliams's *Charles W. Chesnutt and the Fictions of Race* (Athens: U of Georgia P, 2002), a defining work emphasizing the importance of language in Chesnutt's fiction both as an idiom used to construct race and in terms of black vernacular as a signifying system.

NOTES

1. This and other references are to *The Journals of Charles W. Chesnutt,* ed. Richard Brodhead (Durham: Duke UP, 1993).
2. Charles W. Chesnutt, *Paul Marchand, F.M.C.,* ed. and intro. Dean McWilliams (Princeton, NJ: Princeton UP, 1999).
3. Charles W. Chesnutt, *Mandy Oxendine,* ed. Charles Hackenberry, foreword by William Andrews (Urbana and Chicago: U of Illinois P, 1997).
4. Charles W. Chesnutt, *Evelyn's Husband,* ed. Matthew Wilson and Marjan A. Van Schaik, introduction by Matthew Wilson (Jackson: U of Mississippi P, 2005).

Acknowledgments

We would like to acknowledge those who have assisted us in one way or another during the course of preparing this collection. We want to express our appreciation for the continued support of Dr. Alma Vinyard and the English faculty and staff of Clark Atlanta University. We thank the administration and staff of the Atlanta University Center Robert W. Woodruff Library for research assistance and technical services. We thank Marita Lambert for her assistance in our initial preparation of the manuscript. We are grateful to friends and family for their support and interest in our collection. A special note of thanks is extended to William Glass for his steadfast encouragement and inspiration.

Finally, we would like to thank the contributors of the collection for their exceptional scholarship and commitment to this project.

Passing in the Works of
CHARLES W. CHESNUTT

Charles W. Chesnutt's Historical Imagination

Werner Sollors

In the past decade or so we have witnessed the republication of pretty much all of Charles W. Chesnutt's collected and uncollected works and the first printed editions of his unpublished journal, novels, and selected correspondence. (Richard Brodhead, William Andrews, Joseph McElrath et al., Ernestine Pickens, SallyAnn Ferguson, Nancy Bentley, Sandra Gunning, Dean McWilliams, Matthew Wilson, and Judith Jackson have recently edited Chesnutt's works.) Eric Sundquist's study *To Wake the Nations* devotes a third of the book, a total of about two hundred pages, to Chesnutt—more than to W.E.B. Du Bois or to any other author. Numerous new and younger critics have joined the ranks of established Chesnutt scholars, and at a recent American Literature Association meeting Chesnutt may well have been the single most popular American writer, judging by the many papers that were devoted to his work. How can one account for this remarkable revival? What I would like to do is to address Chesnutt's extraordinary sense of the history that he was living and that lay behind him. It is my feeling that Chesnutt's historical imagination, paired with his sense of irony, made him an unusually perceptive witness of his own time. I say "unusual," for the main drift of early African American literature was *not* historical. The previous sentence seems hard to believe, written at a time when historical fiction has become a dominant genre in African American writing, with slavery one of its central themes. But it appears that from 1853 to 1941, a period during which historical fiction was very popular in the Western world, only *one* truly historical African American novel was published: Arna Bontemps's *Black Thunder* (1935). And this book may have come out of the Popular Front's interest in the slave rebel motif that the Comintern (Communist International) encouraged writers on the Left to represent. The reasons for the paucity of a specifically African American historical imagination in the form of historical fiction have never been fully accounted for. One thing seems clear: major black writers (perhaps with the exception of Paul Laurence Dunbar in a few of his poems) have not easily been able to make themselves look back at the past with a sense of nostalgia. For most writers, slavery's memory may have been too painful, too embarrassing, too formidable an obstacle to permit the full development of a backward glance; also, of course, each writer's own present contained many urgent social problems—segregation, disfranchisement, discrimination—that needed to be addressed. Furthermore, writing centrally, honestly, and with the wisdom of hindsight about slavery might make African American authors appear "bitter" in the eyes of their readers. Thus it is no coincidence that Booker T. Washington's autobiography, *Up from Slavery,* contains numerous explicit assertions that the author is *not* bitter; of course, he also offers the most straightforward "from-to" American progress narrative as the shape of his autobiographic history.

Chesnutt was keenly aware of the problems of remembering slavery when he wrote his biography of *Frederick Douglass* (1899), newly edited by Ernestine Pickens in 2001. Chesnutt describes how Douglass "beheld every natural affection crushed when inconsistent with slavery, or warped and distorted to fit the necessities and promote the interests of the institution." And he mentions "the strokes of the lash," "the wild songs of the slaves" beneath which Douglass read "the often unconscious note of grief and despair" (15–16). Chesnutt emphasizes that Douglass perceived "the debasing effects of slavery upon master and slave alike" (16). Yet Chesnutt continues in a manner that might surprise contemporary students of American and African American literature who most frequently read Douglass's 1845 narrative. Here is Chesnutt's comment: "Doubtless the gentle hand of time will some time spread the veil of silence over this painful past; but while we are still gathering its evil aftermath, it is well enough that we do not forget the origin of so many of our civic problems" (16). Interestingly, Chesnutt gives far more emphasis to Douglass's life as a free man and devotes only the first two of a total of twelve chapters to Douglass's experiences as a slave. Adding a touch of irony that showed his acute sense of topics generating nervousness at the time he wrote the biography, Chesnutt also wondered why Douglass's white father "never claimed the honor, which might have given him a place in history" (13). How could a writer deal with a painful past that hopefully, one day, would be forgotten, but that needed not to be forgotten *yet*—as it was "the origin of so many of our civic problems"? How could the historical trauma of slavery be represented so that its continuing effect on the gilded age and fin-de-siècle would become apparent? This seems to be the task Chesnutt himself; and Chesnutt's conjure tales (many were collected in *The Conjure Woman* [1899], the same year as the Douglass biography) come closest to representing fully the troubling legacy of the recent history of slavery in the period of Reconstruction and thereafter. Take the example of "Dave's Neckliss" (though it is not, in fact, included in *The Conjure Woman* and was first republished by Sylvia Lyons Render, a true pioneer of Chesnutt studies). It is the powerful story of a slave who symbolically turns into the ham that his master had fastened to his neck as a punishment for his having supposedly stolen ham. Yet strangely, this version of the curse of Ham works like a "cha'm" that gives Dave a reified identity, an identity he can no longer shed. As Uncle Julius, the living witness of slavery times, reports:

W'en de ham had be'n tuk off'n Dave, folks kinder stopped talkin' 'bout 'im so much. But de ham had be'n on his neck so long dat Dave had sorter got use' ter it. He look des lack he'd los' sump'n fer a day er so atter de ham wuz tuk off, en did n' 'pear ter know w'at ter do wid hisse'f. (*Stories, Novels, and Essays* 729)

Dave ends up hanging himself in the smokehouse, thus symbolically *becoming* the ham. From a literary point of view, this is a moment at which Chesnutt's realistic writing strategy seems to reach a breaking point and begins to sound thoroughly modernist. Dave's metamorphosis is less an echo of Ovid than an anticipation of Kafka or Faulkner or the magical realists. For Chesnutt's purposes as a writer, fictionalizing a specific history, telling a magical, harrowing story seemed the appropriate way of offering a version of history as suffering. The core of his conjure tales always lies in the pain of the slave experience (Henry is subject to fluctuating prices, Po' Sandy to systemic instability, Sis' Becky to separation of mother and child, and so on). And the dreamlike, magical quality of these folk and pseudo-folk tales (made up by Chesnutt "in the manner" of folk) forces the reader in a seemingly indirect way to confront the painful past. Some of Annie Sullivan's reactions to the stories suggest this effect; thus she responds to Julius's telling of the inside tale of "Po' Sandy," a "gruesome narrative" to which she listened "with strained attention": "What a system it was . . . under which such things were possible!" (*Stories, Novels, and Essays* 28). Chesnutt knew only too well, of course, that this, in the 1890s, was not the reaction one could hope for among most readers. He complicates the form of fictionalizing the past by embedding the inside tale into the popular form of a frame narrative in which Chesnutt lets the northern, progress- and enterprise-oriented, first-person-singular narrator John keep his distance from Julius's vivid stories of the past. Here is one of the many descriptions John offers of Julius:

His curiously undeveloped nature was subject to moods which were almost childish in their variableness. It was only now and then that we were able to study, through the medium of his recollection, the simple but intensely human inner life of slavery. His way of looking at the past seemed very strange to us; his view of certain sides of life was essentially different from ours. He never indulged in any regrets for the Arcadian joyousness and irresponsibility which was a somewhat popular conception of slavery; his had not been the lot of the petted house-servant, but that of the toiling field-hand. While he mentioned with a warm appreciation the acts of kindness which those in authority had shown to him and his people, he would speak of a cruel deed, not with the indignation of one accustomed to quick feeling and spontaneous expression, but with a furtive disapproval which suggested to us a doubt in his own mind as to whether he had a right to think or to feel, and presented to us the curious psychological spectacle of a mind enslaved long after the shackles had been struck off from the limbs of its possessor. (*Stories, Novels, and Essays* 722)

This would seem to remind the reader of stories like Dave's, but before the reader too readily agrees with John, Chesnutt lets his frame narrative continue:

Whether the sacred name of liberty ever set his soul aglow with a generous fire; whether he had more than the most elementary ideas of love, friendship, patriotism, religion,—things which are half, and the better half, of life to us; whether he even realized, except in a vague, uncertain way, his own degradation, I do not know. I fear not; and if not, then centuries of repression had borne their legitimate fruit. But in the simple human feeling, and still more in the undertone of sadness, which pervaded his stories, I thought I could see a spark which, fanned by favoring breezes and fed by the memories of the past, might become in his children's children a glowing flame of sensibility, alive to every thrill of human happiness or human woe. (*Stories, Novels, and Essays* 722–723)

In the form of Chesnutt's stories there are then always at least two conflicting views of the past; in fact, more than two if we include the often sympathetic Annie and some minor characters. What the stories stress is that the interpretation of the meaning of the past for the present is what matters. Furthermore, Chesnutt asks the reader to note the ambivalence in Julius: Should we detect, as Douglass did, an "often unconscious note of grief and despair" or, as John does, view Julius's stories as governed by ulterior motives? And since John is the ultimate narrator, this raises the important question of how reliable or unreliable a frame narrator John really is. Has the past really passed, has the old order of slavery given way to a new hopeful beginning, or are John and Julius reenacting a version of the master-slave relationship under the new rules of "freedom"? Chesnutt's conjure tales may thus be considered not only as historical fiction but also as a short story cycle which makes the interpretation of the past vital for an understanding of the present.

I have thus far focused on a few of the most familiar conjure tales but should add briefly that Chesnutt also *did* write an African American historical novel before Bontemps. *Paul Marchand, F.M.C.*, written in 1921, but first published in Dean McWilliams's edition in 1999, may well be the first African American historical novel. More than that, it was written with a very sophisticated and self-conscious understanding of the genre, an understanding that anticipates some of the points György Lukács would later make about the genre of the historical novel. Listen to the beginning of the novel, the first sentence of the foreword: "The visit of a French duke to New Orleans, in the early part of the last century, and the social festivities in his honor, are historical incidents" (3). From this point, Chesnutt moves forward to discuss the probability of a story like the one he is telling and continues: "The quadroon caste vanished with slavery, in which it had its origin. Indeed long before the Civil War it had begun to decline. Even the memory of it is unknown to the present generation, and it is of no interest except to the romancer and the historian, or to the student of sociology, who may discover some interesting parallels between social conditions in that earlier generation and those in our own" (3–4).

Chesnutt uses the historical setting of New Orleans in the 1820s, of course, to get to the core experience of Paul Marchand, F.M.C., who turns out actually to be white heir Paul Beaurepas. It is the experience of seeing the world both from a white and a non-white point of view, when his "quadroon training pushed itself to the front"—and this permits Paul to feel a kind of pity he could not have felt had he looked at life as a white man only. Perhaps one can say that the thrust of Chesnutt's historical fiction was to convey a sense of "quadroon training" to his readers in a racially polarized society.

Lionel Trilling, in his essay "Art and Fortune" (1948), included a longer footnote in which he wondered, but ultimately doubted, whether ethnicity and race provided an American substitute, or equivalent, for the function of class in the European novel of manners. Briefly mentioning the case of American attitudes toward minorities such as blacks or Jews, Trilling answers his question in the negative, since there is

no real cultural struggle, no significant conflict of ideals, for the excluded group has the same notion of life and the same aspirations as the excluding group, although the novelist who attempts the subject naturally uses the tactic of showing that the excluded group has a different and better ethos; and it is impossible to suppose that the novelist who chooses this particular subject will be able to muster the satirical ambivalence toward both groups which marks the good novel even when it has a social *parti pris.* (253)

I think that one can responsibly argue that Chesnutt is precisely the American writer who manages to sustain an ambivalence toward two groups in the drama he presents, in which he succeeded because of very carefully devised formal structures (including such features as a carefully balanced frame narrative opening up multiple ironies). Furthermore, his work suggests a significant cultural struggle between the magical memory in the world of the ex-slave and the spirit of modernization—while retaining a "satirical ambivalence" toward both. Chesnutt also explicitly saw "caste" in the sense of racial difference as the American novelist's equivalent to the European tradition of caste in the sense of social class. Viewing his own role as a writer in historical terms, Chesnutt reflected on this issue very much in a proto-Trillingian fashion: Chesnutt wrote in his now famous essay "Post-bellum—pre-Harlem,"

Caste, a principal motive of fiction from Richardson down through the Victorian epoch, has pretty well vanished among white Americans. Between the whites and the Negroes it is acute, and is bound to develop an increasingly difficult complexity, while among the colored people themselves it is just beginning to appear. (*Stories, Novels, and Essays* 912)

Perhaps it is not surprising that Chesnutt's time has finally come.

WORKS CITED

Chesnutt, Charles W. *Charles W. Chesnutt: Stories, Novels, and Essays.* Ed. Werner Sollors. New York: Library of America, 2002.
———. *Frederick Douglass.* Ed. Ernestine W. Pickens. Intro. William L. Andrews. Atlanta: Clark Atlanta UP, 2001.
———. *Paul Marchand, F.M.C.* Ed. and Intro. Dean McWilliams. Princeton: Princeton UP, 1999.
Trilling, Lionel. *The Liberal Imagination: Essays on Literature and Society.* Garden City: Anchor, 1953.

Signifying the Other
Chesnutt's "Methods of Teaching"

SALLYANN H. FERGUSON

On Thursday evening, November 23, 1882, at the second annual convention of the segregated black North Carolina Teachers Association in Raleigh, North Carolina, twenty-four-year-old Charles W. Chesnutt delivered a speech entitled "Modern Methods of Instruction," and when he had finished, around ten o'clock, the session was adjourned. The paper appeared in print the following year as part of the association's annual minutes with its title changed to "Methods of Teaching." While Chesnutt's essay reads like a scholarly treatise celebrating the achievements of certain European intellectuals and their work, its misquotations, inclusions, and omissions signal the impact of nineteenth-century racial politics on the public utterances of this budding short story writer, novelist, and essayist. As he surveyed various teaching theories and methods developed by ancient and modern Eurocentric thinkers, Chesnutt subtly altered their ideas to fit his subtext of African American educational expansion. Such subversive navigation around the racial Other,[1] a long-standing practice with Chesnutt in both literature and life, freed him to put on oral and written performances that simultaneously catered to the disparate cultural needs and expectations of the association's unusual racially mixed audience—integrated that particular night by the racist white North Carolina governor Thomas Jarvis and his cohorts. Indeed, a careful study of Chesnutt's language in "Methods of Teaching" suggests not only that he maneuvered around presumed threats to already besieged Southern black educational programs, but that, in the process, his signifying double-voice also established an early, nonfictional model for a variety of similar fictional educational masqueraders in the presence of racist Others. Inspired by such teaching mentors as brothers Robert and Cicero Harris and professor/orator Joseph C. Price, Chesnutt himself provides an early prototype for such later fictional educators as J. Saunders Redding's Perkins Thomas Wimbush in *Stranger and Alone* (1950) and Ralph

Ellison's A. Hebert Bledsoe in *Invisible Man* (1952), whose signifying personalities and behaviors are hallmarks of the African American literary tradition.

Before Charles W. Chesnutt took the podium in Raleigh that evening, he had been well schooled by diverse instructors in a wide variety of educational subjects and teaching techniques. Certainly, as biographer Frances Richardson Keller observes, "Whatever the means, whatever the dangers, Chesnutt's freeborn parents [Ann Maria Sampson Chesnutt and Andrew Jackson Chesnutt] transmitted a thirst for knowledge to their son Charles. It stayed with him all his life" (30). This early parental tutelage—especially from his mother—gave way to Chesnutt's decades-long association with the Richardson and Harris families, who, like his own family before the Civil War, had emigrated from the economically and socially depressing environment of Fayetteville, North Carolina, to the promise of Ohio, only to return to their Southern homeland when the postbellum era seemed to augur better opportunities and security.² Constance E. H. Daniel identifies "a bright thread of aggressiveness and high purpose" in the histories of the Richardsons and Harrises and explains: "Wherever they have gone, these families have been in the vanguard of Negro progress. From them has come an impressive line of educators, reformers and leaders in political and civic life" (3). Another historian, Earle H. West, also documents how—with the occasional sponsorship of the American Missionary Association and the Freedmen's Bureau—William, Robert, Cicero, and other Harris relatives brought their energy to various parts of Virginia and North Carolina. By 1865 Robert, whose teachings were to influence Chesnutt the most, had relocated to Fayetteville, where he organized and taught at day, evening, and Sabbath schools in town, as well as at satellite schools in rural areas. He often staffed the latter with students imbued with his own educational philosophy, one that combined scholarly excellence with religious piety.³ According to Keller, "Harris noticed the abilities of a boy in his classes. The encouragement and direction he gave that boy—Charles Waddell Chesnutt—proved a powerful influence in Chesnutt's life" (37). In fact, after Robert Harris's untimely death in 1880, the future author became the second principal of the State Colored Normal School, which was co-founded by Harris as the Howard School in 1877 and is today Fayetteville State University.⁴

In an essay entitled "Joseph C. Price, Orator and Educator: An Appreciation," Chesnutt honors another mentor who inspired him to understand and even revere the power of oratory as advocacy, declaring that it "has never been an art that is practiced primarily for its own sake [but] has always been associated with some cause—good or bad, according to the viewpoint" (*Essays and Speeches* 556). Though a youthful contemporary only four years his senior (rather than ten years older, as Chesnutt mistakenly claims in the text), Price was an accomplished platform fighter who drew the author's attention and praise precisely because he "distinguished himself as orator and advocate" (556) by using "a clear exposition of his views in a magnetic voice" (557) for a worthy purpose, namely, "to assist in raising funds for this school [Livingstone College]" (558). More significantly, Chesnutt admired "Dr. Price's good sense and diplomacy . . . for it requires good sense, diplomacy and some self-restraint for a colored man to discuss the race problem without saying some things which white people would not like, however true they might be" (559).

Throughout "Methods of Teaching," Chesnutt displays considerable rhetorical diplomacy through a double-voice that challenges the profound inferiority complex that historically rendered Euro-Americans economically and psychologically dependent upon the suffering of colored peoples, regardless of white protestations to the contrary. Indeed, early in "Joseph C. Price," the author characterizes the platform speaker's challenge, saying that Price was born "at a very opportune time" for healing racial divides, except that "it was perhaps too much to expect of poor human nature that the former masters should not resent the enforced equality before the law of their former slaves" and hence develop "a feeling . . . that they must keep the Negroes down politically and socially and a conviction on the part of many Negroes that they cannot safely trust their Constitutional rights in the hands of the white South" (554). White racists especially resented African Americans like Price and Chesnutt, who, as Richard Brodhead notes, "exemplifie[d] a group coming to social identity in the postbellum decades that can variously be labeled the black intelligentsia, the black bourgeoisie, or the black professional class" (15).

In a journal entry dated January 21, 1881, the author shows a profound understanding of this white racial insecurity when he recounts a conversation his African American friend Robert Hill of Fayetteville had with a white Southerner named John McLaughlin, who cannot control his racial insecurity after Hill describes Chesnutt as a gentleman and scholar. McLaughlin asks, "'Does he think he's as good as a white man[?]'" and then answers his own question with, "'Well he's [Chesnutt's] a nigger; and with me a nigger is a nigger, and nothing in the world can make him anything else but a nigger'" (160–161). Further illustrating that whites generally rely on racism to elevate themselves psychologically above more socially accomplished and competitive blacks like himself, Chesnutt remarks, "[That] reminds me of the sentiment expressed by an old poor white beggar, who was at the time eating scraps in a colored man's kitchen[:] 'Well, for his part, let other people think as they please, he always did like niggers as long as they kept in their place, and he wasn't ashamed to say so either.'" Chesnutt adds that McLaughlin "'embodies the opinion of the South on the 'Negro Question'" (161). Since assertive blacks had greater proximity to Caucasian people through the marketplace, they were more likely to encounter and be discomfited by the discrimination whites incessantly relied upon to bolster their ever-sagging self-esteem. Thus, about a year after Joseph Price had also addressed an integrated audience of "the greatest [white and colored people] assembled in the state . . . on a plane of civic equality" (*Essays and Speeches* 559), the pacifist Chesnutt—like several clever protagonists who people Chesnutt's short stories, such as "The Passing of Grandison" and "Baxter's Procrustes"—did not "storm the [Raleigh] garrison" but won racial battles as his role models did, with mocking rhetorical eloquence.

To promote his theme of educational expansion for Southern black children while not appearing to say "some things which white people would not like, however true they may be," Chesnutt, throughout "Methods of Teaching," semantically reconstructs the "term *education* . . . [from] the narrowest and most generally accepted use" (*Essays and Speeches* 40). Meticulously, he complicates the rhetorical structure of the essay by first paraphrasing and then enclosing within quotation marks his redefinitions so that they seem to be authoritative direct citations from the European intellectuals whose names grace his speech. For instance, Chesnutt writes, "'History . . . is philosophy teaching by example'" (41), a revision of the similar epigram, "History is philosophy from examples," the original source of which is *Ars Rhetorica*, by Dionysus of Halicarnassus (ca. 30–70 B.C.). With studied misquotation and misleading punctuation, he piggybacks on and expands the Dionysian view of history from an essentially static body of knowledge for general instruction to a more democratic and fluid teaching methodology as relevant "to education as to government, or arts, or morals, or any department of life" (41). Indeed, the author linguistically redefines history itself, also declaring it pedagogy equally capable of the "drawing out or unfolding of all the faculties of intellect, body and conscience or the moral sense, in a harmonious and well-balanced development, giving to each faculty its due proportion of training, regarding no one attribute of the man as superior, but holding each to be supreme in its sphere, and all equally necessary to a perfect whole" (40–41).[5] Thus, to execute his philosophy of education, Chesnutt employs the logical fallacy of worth and value by association—a traditional black survival technique—and turns his discussion of Socrates, Plato, Aristotle, Shakespeare, Martin Luther, Wolfgang Ratich, the Pietists, Kant, Locke, and many others into a survey of representative European teaching methodologies that conveniently accord with his own black American covert academic agenda.

John Sekora describes how slave narrators achieved a comparable validation of their perspectives through a similar method of linkage, especially noting "the feared power of words and the length to which [slave] owners [and slaves alike] would dissemble in order to construct and control a master text of their own lives" (485). In his postbellum world, Chesnutt presumes that "[one] could keep his life [at Fayetteville] intact" (Sekora 485) when he makes it appear that European master texts implicitly authenticate a minority educational program to which Chesnutt feared a majority culture might now be inclined to reduce allotments. According to historian Percy Murray, "One of the difficulties for black education in the 1880s was funding.... [T]here were tremendous differences between funding for the University of North Carolina at Chapel Hill and the black normal schools" (18). Historian Frenise Logan further highlights this problem by noting that until 1885, the white-dominated state government attempted to keep an 1875 constitutional commitment to maintain separate but equal educational facilities, but after 1885 "North Carolina was beginning to manifest a tendency already well established by that date in other southern states—a capitulation to the popular white feeling against Negro education" (140).[6] In an 1892 *Nation* article, Harvard educator Albert Bushnell Hart wrote that a "public man of intelligence" said that North Carolina's whites "don't want the Negroes to get educated, or to get rich, the more educated they are, the worse it is for us. It is a big stick in their hands" (qtd. in Logan 140). Surely Chesnutt's momentarily integrated audience of Southern blacks and whites at the black teachers' state convention must have been impressed with his Joseph Price–like eloquence, albeit for different reasons. The African American listeners, who were not just classroom teachers but, as the Constitution of the Teachers Association allowed, "any person . . . actively interested in Negro education in North Carolina" (Murray 138), must have rejoiced at seeing an erudite black man eloquently advocate for more educational opportunities for black people. The insecure whites must have been just as proud to hear Chesnutt cater to "the master's compulsion . . . [to have] the slave . . . authorize the master's power" (Sekora 485) by paying homage to their European intellectual heritage.

Chesnutt also misquotes the Bible in "Methods of Teaching," using religion to fortify his narrative voice with its moral authority even as he interrogates its historic educational blunders. To emphasize that the growth of the papal system in the early church "caused ignorance and superstition to settle like a nightmare over the face of Europe and brought on the period of a thousand years of mental and moral stagnation known as the Dark Age" (*Essays and Speeches* 43) and, by extension, to suggest a similar prospect for the United States if black education is neglected, Chesnutt writes that the church considered learning "'strong meat, not fit for babes'" (43). The full biblical verse reads: "But strong meat belongeth to them that are of full age, *even* those who by reason of use have their senses exercised to discern both good and evil" (Hebrews 5:14). The author's misquotation in the first part of the sentence does not alter its essential meaning about *when* one should be taught—at "full age"—but it does draw attention to the second half of the line— "*even* those who by reason of use have their senses exercised to discern both good and evil"—that he leaves out. The very absence of these words implies that, like the early Christian church, Southern authorities risk an era of cultural drought similar to the Dark Ages of Europe if they continue to boost their sense of supremacy at the expense of the wasted black mind. By underscoring through omission *who* gets educated or not, Chesnutt seeks a remedy that embraces "*even those*" masses of illiterate African Americans starving for formal instruction from the members of the North Carolina Teachers Association and their supporters. Such rhetorical indirection remains consistent with Price's truth-telling goals and practices and Chesnutt's own moral determination to use literature to rid whites of their prejudices.[7] In a journal entry dated May 29, 1880, and especially in later essays, the author stated that he would not confront the "race" problem directly, in print or otherwise, for "the [American racist] garrison will not capitulate: so their position must be mined, and we will find ourselves in their midst before they think" (140). Accordingly, signifying literary stealth pervades Chesnutt's work to such an extent that critic David D. Britt subtitled an analysis of the author's conjure tales "What You See Is What You Get." Its presence in "Methods of Teaching" highlights this author's seminal role in early discussions about black education in a racist land, an aspect of his professional life scholars have yet to examine closely.

Toward the end of "Methods of Teaching," Chesnutt sets in direct quotation marks a long paraphrase of teaching theories developed by the Swiss educator John Henry Pestalozzi (1746–1827) that William C. Woodbridge summarized in the essay "The Pestalozzian System of Education," which first appeared in the *American Annals of Education and Instruction for the Year 1837*. By the early nineteenth century, Euro-Americans like Woodbridge had already begun to translate into English Pestalozzi's educational principles expressed in such texts as *How Gertrude Teaches Her Children* (1801). Chesnutt apparently discovered Woodbridge's essay either in *American Annals* or in *Pestalozzi and Pestalozzianism: Life, Educational Principles, and Methods of John Henry Pestalozzi with Biographical Sketches of His Several Assistants and Disciples* (1859), where it was reprinted by Henry Barnard.[8] Evidence that Woodbridge's essay is indeed Chesnutt's source in "Methods of Teaching" shows when he reproduces—sometimes almost verbatim—the very same ideas that Woodbridge outlines in two sections titled "General Principles of Pestalozzi" and "Defects of the Pestalozzian System."[9] After noting that "Pestalozzi assumed as a fundamental principle, that education, in order to fit man for his destination, must proceed according to the laws of nature" (8), Woodbridge writes:

1.   . . . he [Pestalozzi] sought . . . to develope [*sic*], and exercise, and strengthen the faculties of the child by a steady course of excitement to self-activity, with a limited degree of assistance to his efforts.

2. . . . he endeavored to find the proper point for commencing [an educational system], and to proceed in a slow and gradual, but uninterrupted course, from one point to another—always waiting until the first should have a certain degree of distinctness in the mind of the child, before entering upon the exhibition of the second. . . .

3. . . . he opposed the undue cultivation of the memory and understanding, as hostile to true education. He placed the essence of education, in the harmonious and uniform development of every faculty, so that the body should not be in advance of the mind, and that in the development of the mind, neither the physical powers, nor the affections should be neglected; and that skill in action should be acquired at the same time as with knowledge. . . .

4. He required close attention and constant reference to the peculiarities of every child, and of each sex, as well as to the characteristics of the people among whom he lived, in order that he might acquire the development and qualifications necessary for the situation to which the Creator destined him. . . .

5. He limited the elementary subjects of instruction to Form, Number and Language, as the essential condition of definite and distinct knowledge; and believed that these elements should be taught with the utmost possible simplicity, comprehensiveness and mutual connection.

6. . . . he thought the things perceived of less consequence, than the cultivation of the perceptive powers, which should enable the child to observe completely. . . .

7. He maintained that every subject of instruction should be properly treated; and thus become an exercise of thought. . . .

8. Pestalozzi . . . attached great importance to Arithmetic, particularly to Mental Arithmetic. . . . He also introduced Geometry into the elementary schools, and the art connected with it, of modeling and drawing beautiful objects. . . .

9. He aimed at a development of the laws of language from within . . . which would not only cultivate the intellect, but also improve the affections. . . . Pestalozzi introduced vocal music into the circle of school studies, on account of its powerful influence on the heart. . . .

10. He opposed the abuse that was made of the Socratic method in many of the Philanthropinic and other schools. . . .

11. Pestalozzi opposes strenuously the opinion that religious instruction should be addressed exclusively to the understanding; and shows that religion lies deep in the hearts of men, and that it should not be enstamped from without. . . . [R]eligion should be formally treated of at a later period in connection with feelings thus excited. . . .

12. Pestalozzi agreed . . . that mutual affection ought to reign between the educator and the pupil. . . .

13. Pestalozzi attached as much importance to the cultivation of the bodily powers, and the exercise of the senses as the Philanthropinists. . . . (8)

In "Methods of Teaching," Chesnutt directly cites the core ideas of Woodbridge's summary, reducing it to the following sentence-long citation reiterating that Pestalozzi taught

that education should proceed according to the laws of nature; that it was the duty of the teacher to assist this by exciting the child to self-activity, and rendering him only a limited degree of assistance; that progress should be slow and gradual, but uninterrupted, never passing to a second topic till the first is fully understood; that the memory and understanding should not be unduly cultivated, but all the faculties developed in harmony; that the peculiarities of every child, and of each sex should be carefully studied in order to adapt instruction to them; that the elements of all knowledge were Form, number and Language, and that these elements should be taught with simplicity and thoroughness; that the art of observing should be acquired and the perceptive faculties well developed; that every topic of instruction should become an exercise for the reflective powers; that mental arithmetic, geometry, and the arts of drawing and modeling objects of beauty, were all important exercises for training, strengthening and disciplining the mind; that the laws of language should be developed from within, and the exercises in it made not only to cultivate the intellect, but to improve the affections; that vocal music should be taught in schools, not by note, but by a careful study of the element—any principles of music; that the Socratic method was not suited to young minds, and that in the early stages of instruction, dictation by the teacher and repetition by the scholar is preferable and, at a more advanced stage, the giving out of problems by the teacher, to be solved by the pupil without assistance; that the religious instruction should begin with the mother, the filial feelings of the child should be first cultivated, and directed toward God, and that formal religious instruction should be reserved to a later period, when the child can understand it; that despotic and cruel government in schools was improper, but that mutual affection between pupil and teacher was a better incitement to intellectual activity than prizes or other stimulants to emulation; and, finally that the exercise of the senses and the thorough cultivation of the physical powers were of very great importance to the complete development of the child. (*Essays and Speeches* 45)

Throughout this paraphrase, Chesnutt includes no ellipses to acknowledge numerous missing words, such as his reduction of Woodbridge's "He [Pestalozzi] opposed the undue cultivation of the memory and understanding, as hostile to true education" to "the memory and understanding should not be unduly cultivated." No brackets indicate the myriad rewrites and insertions of his own thoughts, and he deliberately punctuates to give the impression that his synopsis is a verbatim account of Woodbridge's summary. Chesnutt reduces Woodbridge's six-step analysis of the "Defects of the Pestolozzian System" to the one line "The defects of his system were . . ." (9), also introduced and ending with quotation marks that silently integrate his own language with that of the Swiss educator and his American interpreter so that his ideas become virtually indistinguishable from theirs. Nonetheless, before this North Carolina audience, he dares not venture beyond this bold literary amalgamation and address more directly those aspects of Pestalozzi's theories distorted to accommodate America's racist culture, especially the Swiss's belief that "education should proceed according to the laws of nature," which serves as a pretext for the industrial- education-only pedagogy promoted then and, to some extent, now for African Americans. Although highly critical of the anti-intellectualism that pervades the writings of his friend Booker T. Washington, who became the strongest African American proponent of industrial education—a position clearly reflected in books such as *My Larger Education* (1911)—Chesnutt, unlike NAACP leader W.E.B. Du Bois, would not challenge the garrison of Washington's racial accommodation and assert openly that Pestalozzi had this great impact on the education of African Americans. Instead, his paraphrase of Woodridge's "Defects" section states broadly that "modern methods of teaching are all based upon the Pestalozzian theory," a statement he immediately qualifies with the disclaimer, "with such modifications as have been suggested by experience and more advanced knowledge" (9).

Thus, on the surface, Chesnutt's performance of Eurocentric teaching methods appears to be just a benign reading about tedious pedagogues edited for time and space, lacking his usual humorous quips found in other platform readings and deceptively droning on like a monotonous classroom lecture, a smart black man imparting the techniques of European educators to prominent white politicians and African American teachers, administrators, lawyers, preachers, doctors, and journalists (Murray 17). Indeed, Chesnutt mentions the black classroom only once, but his presentation resembles the more sinister fictional speeches delivered later by Perkins Thomas Wimbush, president of Arcadia College, described in J. Saunders Redding's *Stranger and Alone* (1950), as "phenomena of the oratorical art. They were as devious and misleading as a chased fox's tail or as deliberately obscure as the bottom of a well; or they grandiloquently said nothing" (129). Similar to the keynote address Wimbush also gives before a State Negro Teachers Association in *Stranger*, Chesnutt's oration, too, "was many things, did many things. It . . . was arrogant and fawning . . . slanted for black and slanted for white" (129). Redding even pays direct tribute to his signifying literary predecessor and has his power-seeking school superintendent Sheldon Howden agree that Wimbush's appointment as the "first president of a college that wasn't even in existence . . . sounded like something out of a novel by Charles Chesnutt . . . although he [Howden] had never read a Chesnutt novel" (116).

In *Invisible Man* (1952), novelist Ralph Ellison creates an even more perplexing version of Chesnutt's professor prototype in college president Dr. A. Hebert Bledsoe,[10] who chastises the novel's nameless protagonist precisely because he ignores a cardinal principle of black educators and speaks truth to Mr. Norton, a white benefactor and school trustee. When the young man fails to signify in the presence of white money, he causes an outraged Bledsoe to rail: "'Damn what *he* [Norton] wants. . . . Haven't you the sense God gave a dog? We take these white folks where *we* want them to go, *we* show them what *we* want them to see'" (79, emphasis added). Although this student aspires to become like the campus icon of his Southern college, he cannot reconcile himself to this educational duplicity and wonders if "the veil [of ignorance] is really being lifted, or lowered more firmly in place" (28) under such leadership. In fact, instead of learning how to wear a mask for whites from Bledsoe's example, he retains most of his wide-eyed innocence and "[gets] another shock" when, "as we approached a mirror[,] Dr. Bledsoe stopped and composed his angry face like a sculptor, making it a bland mask, leaving only the sparkle of his eyes to betray the emotion that I had seen only a moment before" (79).

Chesnutt's own personal conduct also indicates his firm grasp of the tactics later displayed by Ellison's Dr. Bledsoe and his intention, like Price, to lobby indirectly for his school and himself in a state where conflict between a white quest for both morality and supremacy forced blacks to compete aggressively among themselves for meager educational funds. He became so adept at this task that, during his principalship at Fayetteville, Professor Chesnutt bragged that he enjoyed a personal rapport with state leaders and considered himself favored over other African American educators. In a February 27, 1881, journal entry, he wrote:

A week ago yesterday I was in Raleigh, in the interest of the Normal School: I made a good impression up there, and have been referred to, in the 'News' papers and in debate in the Senate, as "Prof. Chesnutt"; and in the Com[mittee] on Education as a "scholar and a gentleman." [George H.] White and [Alexander] Hicks, [African American educators] from the East, wanted the Normal School moved to Goldsboro or Newbern, and the teachers appointed by the Legislature. But the Com[mittee] supported our school, and took the wind out of White's and Hicks's sails. (162–163)

The author's legislative victory also might have occurred because there was some truth to the rumor that the Fayetteville school was established to train black Democrats—Governor Jarvis's political party—at a time when most African Americans were staunch Abraham Lincoln Republicans. In his last annual report to John C. Scarborough, the State Superintendent of Public Instruction, dated

May 30, 1879, Robert Harris complained in a section entitled "Political Trickery" that "enemies" of the "'baser sort'" were spreading derogatory stories about the State Colored and Normal School and that students were warned of "positive *bodily injury* to compel them to become Democrats" (36). In his annual report the following year, Chesnutt mentions that the agitation against the school had subsided after another attempt to stir it up again (40). Despite Harris's emphatic assertion that the school was "*non-political* and *non-sectarian*" (37) and Chesnutt's claim to being a Republican, they nevertheless received an allocation of two thousand dollars from the racist Democratic officials, much more than the five hundred dollars per annum later granted to each of four similar state normal institutions. Chesnutt's school did not lose any money until 1891—long after he had left North Carolina in 1883—when the state funded a new normal school for blacks at Elizabeth City by taking five hundred dollars from Fayetteville and one hundred dollars each from the four other normal schools established after 1881 (Noble 426).

The African American North Carolina Teachers Association certainly understood Chesnutt's task and method since he was apparently chosen for exhibition before North Carolina's politically connected white bigots precisely because of his ability to articulate the association's educational ambitions. A survey of other convention programs shows that special addresses were reserved for evening sessions, and on that night only two speeches were given: the first by the governor—who Chesnutt acknowledged was a formidable speaker—and the second by Chesnutt. "His Excellency, Governor [Thomas Jordan] Jarvis," holder of the state's purse strings, had "delivered a practical and instructive address" for which the association "returned him a vote of thanks" (Chesnutt, *Minutes* 5), and the author would certainly not follow with any ideas that might upset a mutually beneficial relationship that he, Robert Harris, and the North Carolina State Teachers Association had established with influential whites in Fayetteville and Raleigh. Indeed, because of the economic resourcefulness of local black and white citizens as well as the excellent scholarship of Harris and Chesnutt, Chesnutt was then serving his second term as principal at the Fayetteville school, the first state institution chosen to train African American teachers. Subtly confrontational, his stylistic devices reveal how powerless African Americans historically played up or down to white Others to gain an education, a political strategy practiced with finesse by Chesnutt's favorite slave narrator, Frederick Douglass, who in *Narrative of the Life of Frederick Douglass, An American Slave* (1845) feigns knowledge before his white playmates in order to trick them into teaching him. Thus, one cannot simply dismiss Chesnutt's misquoted paraphrases and omissions as mere evidence of poor editing or misquoting from memory. Nor can he be accused of plagiarism, since his quotation marks indicate no attempt to claim as his own the work of the Other. Indeed, he does just the opposite and, like Douglass, uses the knowledge of white Others to survive them.

NOTES

1. In "'There is plenty of room for us all': Charles W. Chesnutt's America," Carmen Birkle notes that this author's concept of the "foreigner" or "Other" is defined by "language, skin color, geographical origin, myths, and knowledge," all elements "determined by respective cultural backgrounds" (248).

2. See daughter Helen M. Chesnutt's discussion of both the Southern political situation as well as her grandmother Ann Chesnutt's role as teacher in her laudatory biography, especially chapter 1, entitled "North Carolina: Departure and Return" (1–24). In his introduction to the journals, editor Richard H. Brodhead also describes the character of his subject and the political environment into which Chesnutt was born.

3. Frances Richardson Keller and Richard Brodhead also note that Chesnutt was inspired to keep his now-famous journals after Cicero Harris (who later became a bishop in the African Methodist Episcopal Zion Church and helped found Livingstone College in Salisbury, North Carolina) allowed Chesnutt to read his own (Keller 48; Brodhead 9). Whether by accident or design, whites also advanced Chesnutt's education. George H. Haigh, a bookseller who held "strict conservative beliefs in race and class barriers . . . nonetheless opens his bookstore to Chesnutt and converses with surprising candor"; Emil Neufeld, an immigrant German Jewish intellectual, "teaches Chesnutt languages against the counsel of well-placed whites" (*Journals* 4–5 and 141–142).

4. Chesnutt fulfilled his mentors' expectations so well that when the writer decided to reverse the pattern of his parents and return to Cleveland after growing up in Fayetteville, a local newspaper wrote:

> We regret to learn that Mr. C. W. Chesnutt, Superintendent of the State Colored Normal School, has tendered his resignation to the Trustees, having held his position for the past three years with great credit to himself and acceptability to the patrons of the school and the citizens generally. Since the establishment of this institution it has been peculiarly fortunate in the selection of its principals—the first, Robert Harris, whose untimely death was felt as a great loss not only to the school but to the whole community, was a model educator. He was fortunately succeeded by the present incumbent, a man of indefatigable perseverance, whose aim in life has been to excel in all he undertook; and it can be truly said that this school has not faltered in its upward progress under his wise and prudent management. His place will be difficult to fill. (*Fayetteville Observer*, 3)

5. Chesnutt's words are a virtual endorsement of the moral values and educational philosophy that Harris outlined in his annual "Report of the Principal of the State Colored Normal School, for the School Year 1878–79" to Superintendent of Public Instruction John C. Scarborough. Harris wrote: "We aim to prepare better teachers for the public schools; teachers who will know more of the nature of children and their proper development; teachers who understand the subjects to be taught, and good methods for teaching them; teachers who will learn and practice good methods of study and discipline, and, above all, teachers who will, by precept and example, teach the rising generation those principles of virtue and piety by which good characters are formed for time and eternity" (38).

6. Logan also notes that "this constitutional guarantee until 1885 at least was more realized in North Carolina than in most of the former states of the Confederacy" and adds "that the school

official who controlled the school funds before 1885 manifested a genuine desire to be impartial" (140).

7. In "Joseph C. Price, Orator and Educator," Chesnutt recalled an especially stirring event in 1885 at Lincoln Hall in Washington, DC: "After Mr. [Frederick] Douglass and Mr. [Isaiah] Wears had spoken, as Dr. Price was introduced, the audience began to leave, but when his resonant voice sounded out with its opening sentences, the crowd stopped and resumed their seats. He spoke . . . with such eloquence that Mr. Douglass and Dr. Wears met him on his way to his seat and congratulated him, while the audience expressed by their tumultuous applause their appreciation and delight" (561). See also William Jacob Walls's biography *Joseph Charles Price: Educator and Race Leader*, with particular attention to Price's emphasis on educating whites.

8. On page 28 of his volume, Barnard specifically identifies William C. Woodbridge as author of the "summary and comparative view of" Pestalozzi's ideas.

9. Woodbridge's section "General Principles" lists fourteen items and the section "Defects" lists six.

10. In naming Dr. Bledsoe, Ellison is, perhaps, paying tribute to Redding's earlier Dean Bledsoe of Arcadia College, who "could not always get his grammar straight" (111) but understood the role of politics in securing advantage on campus.

Works Cited

Birkle, Carmen. "'There Is Plenty of Room for Us All': Charles W. Chesnutt's America." *Holding Their Own: Perspectives of the Multi-Ethnic Literature of the United States*. Ed. Doreathea Fischer-Hornung and Heike Raphel-Hernandez. Tubingen, Germany: Stauffenburg, 2000.

Britt, Donald. "Chesnutt's Conjure Tales: What You See Is What You Get." *CLA Journal* 15 (1972): 269–83.

Brodhead, Richard H. *The Journals of Charles W. Chesnutt*. Durham: Duke UP, 1993.

Chesnutt, Charles W. "Fayetteville [Colored] Normal School, 1883: Report of the Principal." *Biennal Report of the Superintendent of Public Instruction of NC for the Scholastic Years 1883 and 1884*. Raleigh: Ashe and Gatling, 1884.

———. "Joseph C. Price, Orator and Educator: An Appreciation." *Charles W. Chesnutt: Essays and Speeches*. Ed. Joseph R. McElrath, Robert C. Leitz III, and Jesse S. Crisler. Stanford: Stanford UP, 1999. 554–562.

———. "Methods of Teaching." *Charles W. Chesnutt: Essays and Speeches*. Ed. Joseph R. McElrath, Robert C. Leitz III, and Jesse S. Crisler. Stanford: Stanford UP, 1999. 40–51.

———. *Minutes of the North Carolina State Teachers Educational Association*. Raleigh: Baptist Standard Print, 1883. 5–13.

———. "Report of the Principal of the State Colored Normal School, for the School Year 1879–1880." *Annual Report of the Superintendent of Public Instruction*. Raleigh: P. M. Hale and Edwards, 1881.

Chesnutt, Helen M. *Charles Waddell Chesnutt: Pioneer of the Color Line*. Chapel Hill: U of North Carolina P, 1952.

Daniel, Constance E. H. "Two North Carolina Families—the Harrises and the Richardsons." *The Negro History Bulletin* 13 (1949): 3–12, 14, and 23.

Ellison, Ralph. W. *Invisible Man*. New York: Random, 1952.

Fayetteville Observer. "Resigned." Editorial. June 21, 1883, 3.

Harris, Robert. "Report of the Principal of the State Colored Normal School, for the School Year 1878–79. *Annual Report of the Superintendent of Public Instruction*. Raleigh: P. M. Hale, 1880.

Keller, Helen Richardson. *An American Crusade: The Life of Charles Waddell Chesnutt*. Provo: Brigham Young UP, 1978.

Logan, Frenise A. *The Free Negro in North Carolina, 1876–1894*. Chapel Hill: U of North Carolina P, 1964.

Murray, Percy. *History of the North Carolina Teachers Association*. Washington: National Education Association, 1984.

Noble, Marcus C. S. *A History of the Public Schools of North Carolina*. Chapel Hill: U of North Carolina P, 1930.

Redding, J. Saunders. *Stranger and Alone*. New York: Harcourt, 1950.

Sekora, John. "Black Message/White Envelope: Genre, Authenticity, and Authority in Antebellum Slave Narrative." *Callaloo* 10 (1987): 482–515.

Walls, William Jacob. *Joseph Charles Price: Educator and Race Leader*. Boston: Christopher, 1943.

West, Earle. "The Harris Brothers: Black Northern Teachers in the Reconstruction South." *The Journal of Negro Education* 48 (1979): 126–138.

Woodbridge, William C. "The Pestalozzian System of Education." *American Annals of Education for the Year 1837* 7 (1837): 1–14.

On Flags and Fraternities

Lessons in History in Charles Chesnutt's "Po' Sandy"

M ARGARET D. B AUER

I think South, which I love, and then I think racist, which I hate, and those two
ideas are stuck together in this flag—forever.
—M ARY E LIZABETH of the Lifetime Channel's *Any Day Now*

We come up to the courthouse, and I see the flag waving there. This flag ain't like
the one we got at school. This one here ain't got but a handful of stars. One at
school got a big pile of stars—one for every state.
—J AMES in Ernest Gaines's "The Sky Is Gray"

When Pat Buchanan remarked several years ago that if there is room for "We
shall overcome" in our country, then there is room for the Confederate flag, I
was struck again by the obtuseness of his (and others') failure to see why the
flag flown by an army fighting to preserve slavery (albeit among other issues) is
offensive not only to the descendants of slaves but also to all who find the institution reprehensible—like writer Reynolds Price, for example, who argues against,
simply put, offending others:

As a white native of Warren County, North Carolina, who was born only 68 years
after the end of the Civil War and slavery; as a man who knew several elderly men and
women who had been born slaves; and as the great-grandson of at least one slaveown-
er, I can see no appropriate present use for any of the several Confederate flags outside
a museum or a serious historical film or other dramatic reenactment that makes no
attempt to defend the rebel cause. Perhaps a few generations from now the stain of
slavery, which so appallingly blots the entire Confederate enterprise, will have faded
in its power to offend; but as the direct descendant of many otherwise decent souls
who supported the awful machine of slavery and who defended their holdings against

Union forces, I'd have to say that any present display of the flag in situations other than those named above seems to me a moral insult. (155)

Around the time that Buchanan and others like him began to defend the Confederate flag against those who would have it taken down from state buildings, the mid-1990s, I found myself bringing up the issue of flying the Confederate flag when teaching Charles Waddell Chesnutt's conjure tale "Po' Sandy." In "Po' Sandy," Chesnutt illuminates clearly how a symbol of the Old South—whether it be a kitchen built off of the main house, as in this short story, or a Confederate flag—cannot be separated from the history of slavery and just represent the romantic side of the time period or southern pride. One should neither ignore the not-so-romantic other side of the coin, nor ignore that the "other" side reveals the illusory nature of the romance. As Louis Rubin writes, "There is nothing sentimental or pathetic about the heritage of the Civil War. What it is is *tragic*—people, most of them ordinary, decent people, fighting hard and well for a cause that was basically *wrong*. Thank God it was lost" (46). In her book *Reconstructing Dixie: Race, Gender, and Nostalgia in the Imagined South*, Tara McPherson suggests that, while Americans seem to recognize "the horrors of slavery," "we remain unable to connect this past to the romanticized history of the plantation. . . . The brutalities of those periods remain dissociated from our representations of the material site of those atrocities, the plantation home" (3). Chesnutt's short story illustrates that romanticizing the plantation home goes back at least as far as the nineteenth century—indeed, for as long as romance writers have used the Old South as a setting for their books and entertained readers with their sentimentalized portrayal of that place and time. As Mary Titus points out, Chesnutt's John and Annie, the white Yankee couple in the frame of each of his conjure stories, "bring with them the myths of antebellum life purveyed by popular plantation fiction" (252), which Julius, a former slave, attempts to undermine in the stories he tells for their entertainment (and education).

"Po' Sandy" is the second story in Chesnutt's *The Conjure Woman* (1899). The reader learns in the first story, "The Goophered Grapevine," that John, the white narrator of each story's frame, and Annie, his wife, have recently moved to North Carolina from the North. Subtleties in "The Goophered Grapevine" reveal that although the move was ostensibly made for Annie's health, in reality John's compliance with the doctor's recommendation also allows him to take advantage of the cheap land and labor in the post–Civil War South. Essentially, then, he is a carpetbagger. Chesnutt appears to employ this white character in the tradition of the "authoritative" voice that frames such works as *Narrative of the Life of Frederick Douglass, an American Slave* and Harriet Ann Jacobs's *Incidents in the Life of a Slave Girl*. But rather than validate the narrative to come, in the opening and closing frame of each story of Chesnutt's collection, John attempts to discredit the black narrator of the conjure tales, "Uncle" Julius. The reader soon recognizes, however, that Julius is the true authoritative voice in the collection; like Douglass and Jacobs, he is the actual authority on slavery. So in spite of John's expressions of skepticism at the end of each tale, Julius's stories ring true.

In *The Conjure Woman*'s opening story, the reader learns that Julius is a former slave who still lives on the plantation that John is considering for purchase. The couple meets Julius when John brings Annie to see their potential new home. Julius tells them the first "conjure story" (about the plantation's "goophered" grapevines) to discourage John from buying the vineyard. John is probably not wrong in his assumption that Julius's story of the plantation's conjured crop is motivated by his wish to continue to live free on the land (and off of the remains of the grape crop). But however selfish Julius's motivation for discouraging John's purchase may be, there is much more to Julius's tale than a wish to convince this white man that the crop is bewitched and thus deadly. With this story, Julius begins to "tell about the South": he tries to show with "The Goophered Grapevine," for example, how a slave owner considered his human property as no different from his grape crop.

Readers of Chesnutt have long recognized the Truths about slavery behind the mask of fantastical elements in Chesnutt's stories of men turned into grapevines or, as in "Po' Sandy," into trees. "Po' Sandy" may also be used to remind the twenty-first-century reader, who has read of the horrors of slavery completely unmasked in such works as Toni Morrison's *Beloved*, that there are still other masks that need to be removed—such as the Confederate flag as "a symbol of Southern heritage and tradition and a romantic memorial to the heroism and valor of individual soldiers" (Holmes and Cagle 281–282). Reading Chesnutt's "Po' Sandy" in the context of this more contemporary controversy illustrates Wai Chee Dimock's "Theory of Resonance," showing "why this text might still matter in the present, why, distanced from its original period, it nonetheless continues to signify, continues to invite other readings" (1061). Certainly this reading reveals how "the hermeneutical horizon of [a] text might extend beyond the moment of composition [and] future circumstances might bring other possibilities for meaning" (Dimock 1061).

In the close of "The Goophered Grapevine," John reports that Julius's plan to scare him away did not work: predictably, John disregards Julius's story of a bewitched crop as mere fancy and buys the plantation. Having developed a liking for the old black man, however, John compensates Julius for the loss of the grape crop with a job as carriage driver. Thus does Julius achieve a position from which he will hear what the white man is up to and from which he can educate the

"Yankee" couple about the Old South. Thus, too, does John's position as Julius's employer become reminiscent of the previous owner of this plantation, who was Julius's "master." Therefore, I would argue that John's Yankee "ethnicity" is another mask employed by Chesnutt—in this case, to deconstruct the kind and good-natured, even paternal, southern plantation owner of pre– and post–Civil War plantation fiction that was written in defense of the southern way of life. John certainly becomes, in the course of this collection, a genial but patronizing plantation owner not unlike those who appear in many of Julius's stories.[1]

After "The Goophered Grapevine," "Po' Sandy" begins with John telling the reader that, "for some occult reason," his wife wants a kitchen built off of the plantation house "after the usual Southern fashion" (37–38). John's characterization of Annie's motivation ("some *occult* reason") reflects his failure to understand why she would want a kitchen off of the main house, as opposed to the "very *conveniently* arranged kitchen" *inside* of their house (37, emphasis added). He does, however, inadvertently reveal Annie's motivation when he notes that this new kitchen will be built "after the usual Southern fashion": I would suggest that Annie is setting up her new home in such a way as to play out some Old South fantasy derived from the romantic plantation fiction mentioned previously, a popular genre in her day. When Julius learns that in order to economize on the new kitchen, John plans to use wood from an old schoolhouse on the property— lumber desired by a splinter group of Julius's church for a new church of their own—Julius tells the couple the story of "po'" Sandy. But this tale of a hard-working, favorite slave who once lived—and died—on this very plantation is also told in response to Annie's wish to "rebuild" in "the *usual* Southern fashion." Mary Titus points out that "in the separation of kitchen and house . . . one can read symbolic separations between those who prepare the food and those who consume it" (245–246). Thus, she explains the ultimate motive behind Julius's stories: "Offering them oblique views of slavery's reality, Julius encourages his listeners (and thus Chesnutt encourages his readers) to question romantic representations of plantation life and to reject rather than replicate the antebellum order in their domestic arrangements" (252).

Particularly given the decade during which Chesnutt wrote the conjure stories, the 1890s, it is significant that Julius directs his second story—and most of the subsequent stories—to Annie, a white woman, in particular. According to Cynthia Mills, in her introduction to *Monuments to the Lost Cause: Women, Art, and the Landscapes of Southern Memory*,

ladies' memorial societies formed in the 1860s and 1870s gave way in the 1890s to chapters of the regionwide United Daughters of the Confederacy. Through these groups, female members supported . . . the goals of aging veterans and their sons about how to best justify the South's stubborn stand and stinging loss. Their activism . . . was an important and distinctive element of virtually all Confederate memorialization. (xvi)

In compiling this collection of essays on Confederate monuments (with her co-editor Pamela H. Simpson), Mills found that

one of the most important themes that . . . emerge[d] is the special role played by white women's organizations, who stepped forward to become a significant force in the postwar monument campaigns. Women often took the lead in commissioning Confederate sculptures, decorating buildings, and funding institutions in the hope of preserving a positive vision of antebellum life. (xvi)

Given the role of white women of Chesnutt's era in such activities, which, as Mills points out, "gloss over uncomfortable aspects of the schism between the states, for example the moral and physical violence of slavery" (xv), it is not surprising that the author targets a white woman as the primary audience of his storyteller in many of the conjure tales, beginning with "Po' Sandy" (the white man who intended to purchase Uncle Julius's livelihood being the primary target of the first story, of course). Again, Chesnutt masks his target somewhat in making the woman character a "Yankee"; however, as mentioned previously and as will be discussed further later, romanticizing the Old South in cultural memory is not an exclusively southern activity. Thus, Chesnutt's employment of Annie (and John) reflects the range of his intended audience: all who view the Old South from what Mills terms the "Confederate perspective" (xv), which is the perspective of so much of cultural memory, even before and certainly since *Gone with the Wind*.

In the second tale Julius tells to his new employers, he reports that the "reward" for po' Sandy's industry was that, as his master's children married and moved to homes of their own, this "favored" slave was passed around from one of these places to another so that they could all share him. During one of his tenures at another plantation, Sandy's wife is sold away, but Sandy seems to bounce right back from this loss, for he soon remarries; however, the events that follow reveal to the reader that he has not so easily recovered from losing his first wife. When his new wife, Tenie, admits to him that she is a conjure woman (though she does not practice her "black" magic now that she is a Christian), Sandy asks her to turn him into a tree; as such, he can remain "rooted" to the plantation and, thus, hidden, not have to leave her, too. Sandy's willingness to give up his humanity ironically reveals how very human he is, contradicting the perception that slaves do not feel the kind of familial devotion that white people feel, a view used to justify breaking up families like Sandy's.

Some time after granting Sandy his wish, Tenie is called away to one of the children's plantations to nurse his sick wife. While she is gone, "Sandy" is chopped down for wood to build a kitchen. Upon her return, Tenie is horrified to find a stump where Sandy had stood, the "tree" lying on the ground. She throws herself onto the "body" of the tree in hysterics and must be tied down to keep her out of the way while the "tree" is chopped into boards. With this lumber, the kitchen is built, but eventually none of the slaves except Tenie will go into it after dark because of the "moanin' en groanin' [of] sump'n a-hollerin' en sweekin' lack it wuz in great pain en suffering" (57). Julius reports in wrapping up his tale that the haunted kitchen was eventually torn down and the wood used to build a schoolhouse, which would only be used in the daylight.

Annie is moved by the story of Sandy and Tenie and exhorts John to use new lumber for her kitchen, saying she would never "be able to take any pleasure in that kitchen if it were built out of that lumber" (61). John then closes up this story with the information that soon after the telling of this story, Julius approached Annie for permission to use the old schoolhouse for church meetings. Hearing of Julius's petition confirms John's suspicion that Julius's motive for telling this tale was strictly self-serving. It is apparent to Annie, however, that Julius's stories are about more than filling his own or even his people's needs: she recognizes that he is telling them about slavery. Annie perceives the lesson in the conjure tales, as evident in her remark at the end of this particular one, for example, "What a system it was . . . under which such things were possible!" (60), as well as her later remark at the end of "Sis' Becky's Pickaninny," another story in which family members are sold away from each other, "the story bears the stamp of truth, if ever a story did" (159). Along with Annie, the astute reader recognizes that Chesnutt is subtly deconstructing myths about slavery—revealing, as already noted, for example, what a slave would give up in order to remain with his own family, which undermined myths of blacks not feeling the same as whites about family ties. Even more subtly, in "Po' Sandy" Chesnutt reveals, in disguised but graphic detail, the consequences the runaway slave often suffered upon capture—albeit inadvertently, Sandy is mutilated and ultimately killed for hiding from his duties—but Chesnutt masks the physical abuse of slaves with a magic spell that allows readers to distance themselves (and the white people inflicting the punishment) from the tragic events in the story. The story of Sandy and Tenie apparently takes place somewhere in "Never Never Land," since people cannot actually be turned into trees. The reader can therefore sleep well after finishing this book, as undisturbed as he or she would be after reading a fairy tale. Indeed, as Keith Byerman has suggested of Chesnutt's "Mars Jeems's Nightmare," another story in *The Conjure Woman*, the story might be "too successful in its disguise" (103); Byerman wonders if Chesnutt were so adept at employing white-approved tropes in the collection that he missed the opportunity to educate his turn-of-the-century audience.

Certainly, Annie's husband, John, easily dismisses Julius's stories, in spite of recognizing just before Julius recounts the story of Po' Sandy that, "poured freely into the sympathetic ear of a Northern-bred woman, [Julius's stories] disclose many a tragic incident of the darker side of slavery" (41). Unlike Annie, John does not see this particular story, for example, as anything more than a fairy tale: "Are you seriously considering the possibility of a man's being turned into a tree?" (60), he asks his wife incredulously when she expresses her dismay at the kinds of tragedies that slavery caused. Similarly, at the end of Julius's narration of "Sis' Becky's Pickaninny" several stories later in the collection, John compliments Julius on telling them such an "ingenious fairy tale" (159). In contrast to John's continued grasp of only Julius's pragmatic ulterior motive for telling each story, in the closing frame of "Sis' Becky's Pickaninny," the white couple's exchange about the story Julius has told reveals Annie's recognition of Julius's attempts to educate them. John again remarks upon the implausibility of details in the story—a baby turned into a humming bird and a mocking bird, and a hornet doing the bidding of a conjure woman—to which Annie responds, "Those are mere ornamental details and not at all essential. The story is true to nature and might have happened half a hundred times, and no doubt did happen, in those horrid days before the war" (159). "Sis' Becky's Pickaninny," the fifth in the collection of eight stories, is about the separation of a mother and her baby. This particular "horror" has apparently gotten across to Annie an even fuller understanding of the reality of the antebellum period than did the story of Po' Sandy.

So early in the collection as "Po' Sandy" appears, however, Chesnutt is not yet ready for Annie's full insight into Julius's message. Her reply to John questioning her belief in a story about a man turned into a tree reveals that at that point in the collection she has only partially grasped the message. After placating her husband with "I know the story is absurd . . . and I am not so silly as to believe it," Annie adds, "I think the kitchen would look better and last longer if the lumber were all new" (61–62). Apparently, she still wants the kitchen. Recalling John's early explanation that this kitchen would be "apart from the dwelling-house after the usual Southern fashion" (37–38), the reader should discern the problem with Annie's desire: she still wants to recapture an image she holds of the Old South, in spite of what she has just heard. Annie has apparently missed another motivation Julius has in telling these stories, which is not only to deconstruct myths about slavery but also to de-romanticize the Old South in its entirety.

As suggested previously, Annie's wish to have a kitchen separate from the main house, as was the practice on antebellum plantations to keep possible fires from spreading beyond the kitchen, can be perceived as evidence that she is caught up in and trying to recapture the Old South found in the popular romance novels of the period. Not as practical as her husband, Annie is probably not thinking about protecting the house from fire; rather, she is engaging in some of her own conjuring—she is attempting to conjure up some "moonlight and magnolias," "darkies" singing in the fields, and devoted mammies and menservants, all of which could be found in traditional plantation fiction, which was especially popular with Northern women in the nineteenth century.[2] It is just such a romantic view of the Old South that Chesnutt's story deconstructs. Uncle Julius tells his tales of the slaves who once lived on this plantation, not only to preserve a grapevine for himself or a schoolhouse for the congregation he belongs to, but also to give Annie, especially, a very unromantic perspective on the past.

As demonstrated, "Po' Sandy" is the story of a very devoted, hard-working slave who is "rewarded" for his good service by being sent around from one family member's house to another's and by having his wife sold away while he is gone. This slave chooses to live the life of a tree (which is not so easily uprooted), rather than chance being sent away from his second wife. But he cannot escape his role in life so easily: the tree that is Sandy is cut into planks, which are then used to build a kitchen. Chesnutt is, of course, employing fantastical elements to lighten the horrific events in this story, but the intuitive reader recognizes that he is illuminating how the Old South was literally built by and with the flesh and blood of human beings like Sandy.

When I teach this story, I want the students to recognize that Annie's request for new wood for her old-fashioned kitchen is only halfway to where Julius—and Charles Chesnutt—want her and the reader to be. Furthermore, I wish to show them that the complete lesson to be discerned from this conjure story continues to resonate today if applied to the more recent Confederate flag debates and such recreational activities as Civil War reenactments, Confederate balls, and other like events that romanticize the Old South and the Confederacy. Julius's story "Po' Sandy," like the other conjure tales of this collection, shows that the romantic glamour or even the ideals reflected in the cultural memory of the Old South simply cannot be separated from the history of oppression, which completely undermines the validity of the romance and the possibility of the ideals. As Julius reveals, ironically through fantasy, the horror of that history must be fully recognized if anything is going to be done to rectify the past; the romance is a myth—and a harmful one at that, for its appeal is much more seductive than the disturbing reality. Indeed, Mary Titus has noted, regarding the strong influence of romantic plantation literature on the nineteenth century: "In the battle waged through the second half of the nineteenth century for control over the representation of a remembered South, Charles Chesnutt wrote on the losing side. Romantic plantation fiction and memoir gained primary control of the popular images of southern hospitality for at least a century" (253–254).

Many defenders of the Confederate flag argue that it reflects southern pride and that it is flown in honor of brave Confederate soldiers, rather than in support of the prejudice and racism that led many to fight in the Civil War in order to preserve slavery in the nineteenth century and that continue to motivate white supremacists today.[3] But others argue that it is just that prejudice, that racism, and the institution of slavery from which the flag cannot be separated no matter what the sentiments of an individual who flies it. In his essay "The Confederate Flag and the Meaning of Southern History," Kevin Thornton discusses the attempt to separate the flag from slavery and explains the problem with doing so:

Inherent in the desire to save "heritage," however well-intentioned, is the desire to preserve a pure southern past, a past where honor and glory and a sense of place stand apart, unconnected to racial oppression. There is this desire to separate the nobility of Robert E. Lee from the ignominy of slavery, the man on the horse from the men and women treated as chattel. As understandable (and as politically pragmatic) as this desire is, it is a mistake. Such a position creates a sense of "connectedness" bound only to myth. . . . It seeks to distill an essence of the southern past and southern identity that is unarguably good. But the fact is that Lee's republic was a slave society, and the centrality of that fact should not be de-emphasized if discussions of the Confederacy are to rise above mythology. (240)

Thornton traces "the association of Confederate symbolism with white supremacist feeling" back to the post-Reconstruction era of Jim Crow (236–237), the era in which Charles Chesnutt was writing. In his essay on the history of the Confederate battle flag, John M. Coski traces this attitude in the more recent past: through numerous examples he reveals how once "the looming clouds of civil rights activism grew into a storm that threatened to blow away segregation, the Confederate flag's use as a symbol of white supremacy became explicit" (113). Coski notes that during the era of the Civil Rights Movement, Confederate heritage organizations were ineffective in their attempts "to protect the flag from 'desecration'" by extremist groups like the Ku Klux Klan and the National States' Rights Party (114). He then shows that those who would celebrate the flag's "original [supposedly] noble meaning" in more recent decades have continued to be unsuccessful (115). And finally, he, too, makes an indisputable argument as to why "a symbol of the Confederate cause" cannot be separated from racism:

Confederate nationalists have insisted that the cause was the constitutional principle of states' rights, but during the life of the Confederacy and in the reaction against federal civil rights initiatives, "states' rights" served to preserve the white supremacist status quo. . . . The flag originally was associated with armies whose victories had the effect of preserving a nation which in turn preserved slavery. Subsequently, the

Confederate battle flag was supported by generations of white Southerners who defended Jim Crow segregation. These historical facts made the flag a logical symbol to be dragged into racial controversies. (118)

In a 1996 special issue of *Callaloo* on the Confederate flag, ninety-seven historians present a statement which suggests that "the crux of the present controversy is not in the flag itself but in conflicting interpretations of the Civil War"—referring to those who believe that the Civil War was fought over states' rights. The historians who signed this statement show that the central issue of the war was undeniably to protect the institution of slavery. Their argument is worth quoting in its entirety:

The crux of the present controversy is not in the flag itself but in conflicting interpretations of the meaning of the Civil War. Some South Carolinians deny that the Civil War was fought over slavery, maintaining that it was fought over the rights of the states to control their own destinies. Slavery, they believe, was incidental.

But when South Carolina delegates walked out of the 1860 Democratic National Convention in Charleston as a prelude to secession, their spokesman William Preston minced no words in declaring that "Slavery is our King; slavery is our Truth; slavery is our Divine Right." And a few months later when the signers of the South Carolina Ordinance of Secession issued their Declaration of the Causes of Secession, they specifically referred to the "domestic institution" of slavery. They objected that the free states have "denounced as sinful the institution of slavery." They charged that the free states had "encouraged and assisted thousands of our slaves to leave their homes; and those who remain have been incited by emissaries, books, and pictures, to hostile insurrection."

Moreover, in 1861, as President and Vice President of the Confederate States of America, Jefferson Davis and Alexander H. Stephens each candidly acknowledged that their new nation was created for the specific purpose of perpetuating slavery. In an address to the Confederate Congress in April of 1861, Davis declared that "a persistent and organized system of hostile measures against the rights of the owners of slaves in the Southern States" had culminated in a political party dedicated to "annihilating in effect property worth thousands of dollars." Since "the labor of African slaves was and is indispensable" to the South's production of cotton, rice, sugar, and tobacco, Davis said, "the people of the Southern States were driven by the conduct of the North to the adoption of some course of action to avert the danger with which they were openly menaced." ("Flag," 196–197)

Coski, however, states that "even if historical analysis and argument conclude . . . that the flag's white supremacist overtones are inherent and continuing, it is neither fair nor accurate to attribute racist motives to those who do not accept the argument" (118). Similarly, in Chesnutt's story, Annie's wish to have a kitchen in the Old Southern tradition does not mean that she wants to own slaves or that she would separate family members from each other in order to obtain the perfect servant to work in her kitchen. But if her lifestyle supports the traditional southern "way of life"—which Coski notes was "the rationale for reviving the [Sons of the Confederacy]" (118)—then it does not contribute to ending the oppression of blacks in the South. Simply put by Kevin Thornton, "the emergence of the glorious public memory of the Lost Cause was as inseparable from the birth of Jim Crow as the war was from slavery" (237). Annie's wish to play plantation mistress puts her in the same position as those southerners who, while despising others' violent treatment of slaves, supported (via owning slaves themselves) the institution of slavery that allowed such abuse to go unpunished. And as already noted, buying a plantation and hiring Julius has put John in the position of plantation master not so unlike the master who once owned Julius. Certainly, John's condescending attitude toward Julius is as patronizing as the attitudes of those who supported their participation in the institution of slavery on the basis that blacks needed whites to take care of them.

Chesnutt's stories are full of compassionate slave owners not so unlike John and Annie, yet still the black characters suffer. In the tradition of tragedy, one of Chesnutt's points seems to have been to show how even the slave in the best possible situation—living on a plantation where slaves were seldom beaten—still suffered the horrors of slavery (particularly the separation of family members from each other). Similarly, support of the (false) ideals of the Old South in the post-slavery South led (and leads) to turning a blind eye to the continued abuse and oppression of blacks during Reconstruction (and after). Chesnutt wrote the conjure tales after Reconstruction. He knew that the Confederate way of life had not ended with Lee's surrender and that the South had not been "reconstructed" after the Civil War. He had no way of knowing how long the South would resist change, but his story resonates today as we debate whether the Confederate battle flag should be allowed to fly over courthouses and other state buildings. Tara McPherson suggests that the debate reflects how the flag now "function[s] ... as a visible sign of resistance to a changing South" (33). McPherson illustrates her point by showing how the flag became associated with Jim Crow politics when it was added to the Mississippi state flag in the last decade of the nineteenth century and with integration politics when it was added to the Georgia state flag in the mid-twentieth century, then flown over the South Carolina capitol around the same time (33–34), regarding which Louis Rubin states candidly,

The flag was put there not to honor the memory of the South Carolinians who fought for the Lost Cause of the 1860s, but to rally the defenders of racial segregation during the 1950s. It had been made into a symbol of the Massive Resistance movement, and it stood for the willingness to perpetuate inequality in our own day and time. Its presence did not honor the memory of those who fought the Civil War. (45)

At its worst, as James Forman Jr. points out, the flag has been "used *throughout* [the twentieth] *century* as a symbol by the Klan, Skinheads, and other white supremacists opposed to black demands for equality and constitutional protection" (202, emphasis added). In a similar summation, James C. Cobb notes that by the end of the twentieth century

the Confederate banner had been co-opted by a host of organizations advancing agendas ranging from unabashed white supremacy to militant antigovernmentalism. Southern whites who denied the flag's racist implications could hardly deny that it had been adopted for symbolic purposes by a host of racist hate groups such as the Ku Klux Klan. (140)

This undeniable association of the Confederate flag with racist organizations makes it particularly disconcerting to find such activities as Old South balls (at which, presumably, the Confederate flag is flown) on college campuses. Another contemporary analogy that I bring up when discussing "Po' Sandy" is the Old South ball held by the Kappa Alpha Order at many mainly, but not exclusively, southern universities, so apparently some "Yankees" are still intrigued by the romantic Old South. In a 1966 issue of the *Kappa Alpha Journal* "The Knight Commander's Message" includes a statement of support for such activities:

by resolution of the 44th Convention, the Advisory Council commends as wholesome and edifying the growing tradition in the Order of presenting Old South or plantation balls with appropriate pageantry and costuming. Such functions commemorate and tend to perpetuate the gentle manners and romantic idealism of a gracious and cultivated society. They are in the finest American tradition. We would encourage their extension. ("Knight," 2)

Although I have not inquired directly of the Kappa Alpha Order headquarters on what basis the fraternity continues to defend these balls in the twenty-first century, conversations I have had over the past fifteen years with students who are fraternity members at various universities suggest that the members merely consider the events harmless fun.

   These young men and Kappa Alpha alumni might respond to inquiries about the offensiveness of their balls by asking themselves: Whom does it hurt for fraternity members and their dates to costume themselves in Confederate uniforms and dresses with hoopskirts and hold a ball at a nearby plantation home? James

Forman Jr. shows how such activities *do* harm others: First, he refers to a *Texas Law Review* article by Akhil R. Amar, who points out how Confederate symbols "exclude large numbers of citizens, most notably blacks. The metaphoric exclusion implicit in these symbols is made concrete in the physical exclusion associated with (almost invariably) all-white affairs such as Confederate balls" (qtd. in Forman 202). Then Forman turns to Lee Bollinger's argument (in a *Columbia Law Review* article) that the "thought and message of inferiority, of hatred and contempt . . . is communicated by the discriminatory act and . . . afflicts the human spirit of the victim" (qtd. in Forman 202). It is interesting to note here that to "demonstrat[e] a causal nexus between the harm to the plaintiff and an official display of a Confederate symbol," plaintiffs have "cite[d] *Brown v. Board of Education*, which indicates that harm can include 'feelings of inferiority'" (Martinez 228).

In light of the story "Po' Sandy," I respond to a defense of Confederate balls with a series of questions: Doesn't this occasion continue to promote the false image of the Old South as romantic? Don't these balls serve to segregate the fraternity, or do the African American fraternity members dress up as either slaves or Union soldiers? Thornton's remarks about the exclusive nature of Confederate symbols are interestingly applicable here: "these symbols helped to create, and were from the beginning, symbols of a segregated South. . . . Flags and monuments [and Confederate balls] were deliberate, daily reminders that the kind of history that mattered—public history—happened only to white people" (237).

Issues of fraternity segregation aside, holding a Confederate ball promotes the very same image of the plantation that Charles Chesnutt's conjure stories were written to deconstruct. Annie's realization of the horrors of slavery should lead the reader, if not Annie herself, to the recognition that one cannot evoke the moonlight and magnolias and turn a deaf ear to the "moanin' en groanin'." (Or rather, if one does, he or she becomes a participant in the oppression.) McPherson calls the tendency to "remember and enshrine certain Souths and certain southerners while forgetting others . . . historical amnesia" (5). Worse than such "forgetfulness" is the resentment of remembering that I sometimes encounter in my southern literature courses, reflected in student complaints about the emphasis on race issues in discussions of the assigned readings. And beyond the classroom I have heard complaints often voiced against dredging slavery up whenever affirmative action issues or reparation discussions arise—though I do not recall any public outcry against resurrecting Scarlett and Rhett for a sequel to *Gone with the Wind*.

In her "Theory of Resonance" (mentioned previously), Dimock remarks upon the "topical, circumstantial" readings of a literary text, reminding us that a text could "appear obtuse to future readers who, living among other circumstances and sensitized by other concerns, bring to the same words a different web of meaning" (1061). So, too, then must the instructor on occasion, as I did when teaching this story at Wabash College, a private liberal arts college in the Midwest with an all-male student body. Several times during my year on the faculty there different colleagues—all men—expressed their frustration with sexist remarks made by their students in the classroom and apologized to me in case such remarks were made in my classes. Not surprisingly, my students did not make sexist statements or tell sexist jokes in my hearing. As I pointed out to my colleagues, the students would not want to offend me—they probably meant no offense to their male professors. They just did not realize that a man might—and should—be as offended by a sexist remark as he should be by a racist one, regardless of his race. And keeping in mind that this is an all-male college, in classes with male professors—and the majority of the faculty were male—there were no women to offend; hence, it was "okay" to tell sexist jokes, make sexist statements. Or was it?

This issue provided me with a non-southern analogy to use in teaching "Po' Sandy" that year to my Midwestern students, who were not likely to have Confederate flag license plates or to be interested in donning the Confederate gray for a dance. Uncle Julius led these students to see how even seemingly harmless support of that which signifies oppression—whether a romanticized Old South or a sexist joke—supports continued oppression. I drew an analogy to promoting gender stereotypes in generalizations made about or jokes told at the expense of women, which, intentionally or not, promote, too, traditional perceptions of men—as the natural head of the family and leader of the community, for example—and, thus, the patriarchal system that oppresses not only women but also minorities of either sex. As we consider the seeming harmlessness of Annie's wish to recreate her southern plantation in the physical form she reads about in novels, I ask: Whom is Annie going to hire to cook in that kitchen, to carry the meals to the Big House and serve them to the plantation's new mistress and her family?

Forgetting the service (and suffering) of slaves and their descendents has resulted in the *re*-romanticizing of the Old South by the tourist industry. McPherson shows in *Reconstructing Dixie* how the Old South setting continues to be a source of entertainment, now for tourists of the South. McPherson relates how during a tour of plantation homes, "the 'loveliness' of the homes became the overarching rationale for the tours, as the period's interracial past disappeared along with the history of slavery" (42–43), and she examines various tourist activities that romanticize the Old South. She notes how one Confederate pageant promises to "'transport the audience to the days of long ago . . . that romantic era of the past,'" targeting its advertisement to "'lovers of history and the romantic traditions of the Old South'" (41–42). The history of the Old South, one realizes from this juxtaposition of "history" and "romantic traditions" here, is another "text" whose meaning changes over time. Dimock's "Theory of Resonance" is reflected as well in the problematic endurance and elasticity of this version of history, just as Chesnutt's "Po' Sandy" applies to recent debates over the Confederate flag. And as our cultural memory refocuses on a romanticized Old South, the flags and fraternities—and even some southern studies programs, according to McPherson (11)—ignore or at least overlook the "darker" side of southern history.

Notes

A version of this article originally appeared in *Southern Literary Journal* 40.2 (2008) and is printed here with permission.

1. Kevin Thornton's reminder that slavery was not exclusively southern provides another angle on Chesnutt's choice to have John and Annie come from the North: Thornton points out that Harriet Beecher Stowe recognized that "slavery was an American evil" and attributes her choice of making Simon Legree a native of Vermont to her "not let[ting] the North off the hook" (241). Perhaps Chesnutt, too, is reminding his readers of the shared guilt of white America, North and South, for this institution.

2. It is interesting to note that in the opening frame that introduces the story "Sis' Becky's Pickaninny" John comments upon their new home's "fairly good library" as one source of entertainment (103). Just before Julius's entrance into the story, John notes that he had been "follow[ing] the impossible career of the blonde heroine of a rudimentary novel [and] had thrown the book aside in disgust" (104).

3. For a discussion of the various sides in the Confederate flag debate, see *Confederate Symbols in the Contemporary South*, especially the essay in it by Robert M. Holmes and Christine Cagle. Franklin Forts also provides a succinct characterization of the participants in this debate in an essay, "Living with Confederate Symbols," published in *Southern Cultures* (61). Also see *Callaloo*'s 2001 special issue on the Confederate flag. Though most of the southern contributors to this issue are against the flag being flown because of its offensiveness—like white poet Betty Adcock, who writes, "I believe decency and human feeling should dictate that it not be flown privately, or worn as a badge of either identity or hostility" (1)—most of these same people express their pride in being southern, like black novelist Tina McElroy Ansa, who explains, "I have never thought for a moment that it was the inorganic/heartless/synthetic trappings identified by white Southerners—the Confederate flags, the anthem 'Dixie,' the gray Rebel uniform, the racist license plates, the Rebel yell, the historically incorrect image of plantation life—that tie my heart and soul to the region" (6).

Works Cited

Adcock, Betty. "Some Thoughts on Winds that Move the Flags." *Callaloo* 24.1 (2001): 1–4.

Ansa, Tina McElroy. "What's the Confederate Flag Got to Do with It?" *Callaloo* 24.1 (2001): 5–7.

Byerman, Keith. "Black Voices, White Stories: An Intertextual Analysis of Thomas Nelson Page and Charles Waddell Chesnutt." *North Carolina Literary Review* 8 (1999): 98–105.

Chesnutt, Charles Waddell. *The Conjure Woman*. 1899. Ann Arbor: U of Michigan P, 1969.

Cobb, James C. "'We Ain't White Trash No More': Southern Whites and the Reconstruction of Southern Identity." *The Southern State of Mind*. Ed. Jan Nordby Gretlund. Columbia: U of South Carolina P, 1999. 135–146.

Coski, John M. "The Confederate Battle Flag in Historical Perspective." Martinez et al. 89–129.

Dimock, Wai Chee. "A Theory of Resonance." *PMLA* 112 (1997): 1060–1071.

"The Flag Controversy and the Causes of the Civil War: A Statement by Historians." *Callaloo* 24.1 (2001): 196–198.

Forman, James, Jr. "Driving Dixie Down: Removing the Confederate Flag from Southern State Capitols." Martinez et al. 195–223.

Forts, Franklin. "Living with Confederate Symbols." *Southern Cultures* 8 (2002): 60–75.

Holmes, Robert, and M. Christine Cagle. "The Great Debate: White Support for and Black Opposition to the Confederate Battle Flag." Martinez et al. 281–302.

"The Knight Commander's Message." *Kappa Alpha Journal* (May 1966): 1–2.

Martinez, J. Michael. "Confederate Symbols, the Courts, and the Political Question Doctrine." Martinez et al. 224–239.

Martinez, J. Michael, William D. Richardson, and Ron McNinch-Su, eds. *Confederate Symbols in the Contemporary South.* Gainesville: UP of Florida, 2000.

McPherson, Tara. *Reconstructing Dixie: Race, Gender, and Nostalgia in the Imagined South.* Durham: Duke UP, 2003.

Mills, Cynthia. *Monuments to the Lost Cause: Women, Art, and the Landscapes of Southern Memory.* Ed. Cynthia Mills and Pamela H. Simpson. Knoxville: U of Tennesse P, 2003. xv–xxx.

Price, Reynolds. "A Comment." *Callaloo* 24.1 (2001): 155.

Rubin, Louis D., Jr. "General Longstreet and Me: Refighting the Civil War." *Southern Cultures* 8 (2002): 21–46.

Thornton, Kevin. "The Confederate Flag and the Meaning of Southern History." *Southern Cultures* 2 (1996): 233–245.

Titus, Mary. "The Dining Room Door Swings Both Ways: Food, Race, and Domestic Space in the Nineteenth-Century South." *Haunted Bodies: Gender and Southern Texts.* Ed. Anne Goodwyn Jones and Susan V. Donaldson. American South series. Charlottesville: UP of Virginia, 1997. 243–256.

Passing as Narrative and Textual Strategy in Charles Chesnutt's "The Passing of Grandison"

MARTHA J. CUTTER

Charles Chesnutt's "The Passing of Grandison" (published in *The Wife of His Youth and Other Stories of the Color Line*, 1899) is not properly about "passing" as it was first used in the nineteenth century in the United States, that is, African Americans passing for white or crossing the "color line." As Werner Sollors has argued, the first usage of the term "passing" appears in notices concerning runaway slaves (255). Richard Hildreth's *The Slave; or, Memoirs of Archy Moore* (1836), for example, reproduces an actual advertisement for two runaway slaves which concludes, "I suspect they have taken the road to Baltimore, as Cassy formerly lived in that city. No doubt they will attempt to pass off for white people" (72). In Chesnutt's short story, Grandison passes in a number of ways that this essay will examine, but he never does pass for white. Nor does the story partake of earlier nineteenth-century ideologies that often damned passing as a kind of racial treachery, a base counterfeiting of the self. In Frank Webb's novel *The Garies and Their Friends* (1857), the negative overtones of racial passing are emphasized, as one character comments to another: "It is a great risk you run to be passing for white in that way" (43).[1] But in Chesnutt's story a complicated series of passing acts allows the protagonist to free not only himself, but also his extended family of eight other enslaved individuals.

These are just some of the many ways that Chesnutt's story fools its readers and undermines hegemonic notions of passing, racial identity, and the ability of one individual to "read" another. Texts about passing, such as "The Passing of Grandison," often function on both a narrative and textual level to disrupt constructions of race.[2] On a narrative level, African American characters who assume an identity as white undercut binary divisions between black and white and upset essentialistic notions of racial identity. More importantly, for a writer such as Charles Chesnutt on a textual (or generic/formal) level, stories about passing often pass for something they are not, thereby subverting a reader's way of reading race and of reading texts *about* race; the form of the story itself, in short, constitutes Chesnutt's most intricate act of passing. Furthermore, in Chesnutt's story passing functions on both a narrative level (between characters) and on a textual level (between text and reader) to enact a profound destabilization of constructs of race, identity, and finally of textuality itself. In the end "The Passing of Grandison" illustrates that every reading of a text and every reading of race, like every reading of an individual, must be contextually sensitive, specific to a particular situation, carefully constructed, and continually revised.

PERFORMING SAMBO: NARRATIVE STRATEGIES OF PASSING

We might begin by asking what the term "passing" in the title actually signifies. The central character of the story, a slave named Grandison, does not pass for white, as is common in novels about passing, even those written by Chesnutt himself, such as *The House behind the Cedars* (1900). But Grandison does pass in other ways. Mainly, he pretends to be a contented, happy slave who would never dream of leaving his dear old master. Grandison is taken to the North by his master's son, Dick Owens, who attempts to impress his girlfriend, Charity Lomax, by setting a slave free. But Grandison resists the temptations placed before him by Dick and the abolitionists. In an inversion of a trope common to the slave narrative, when he is kidnapped and taken to Canada, Grandison makes his way back to Kentucky and his master, Colonel Owens, "keeping his back steadily to the North Star" (280–281), much to Colonel Owens's great delight. However, three weeks after his triumphant return, Grandison and eight other individuals (his wife, aunt, uncle, two brothers, mother, father, and sister) escape. Oddly enough, as the narrative voice comments cryptically, "the underground railroad seemed to have had its tracks cleared and signals set for this particular train. Once, twice, the colonel thought he had them, but they slipped through his fingers" (281). Grandison has used his trip to the North and his contacts with abolitionists to engineer the liberation of not just himself, but eight other relatives.

What becomes apparent, then, by the story's end is that Grandison has been skillfully passing as a kind of Sambo-like figure—a contented, ignorant, childlike, happy slave who appears to believe the distorted visions of the world put forward by his white master. He passes so well that even contemporary readers to whom I have taught this text are taken in—and angered—by his Sambo-like persona, a point to which I will return later in the essay. Grandison's exquisite performance of the stereotype is made especially clear by an early incident in which another slave—Tom, Grandison's brother, who is eventually freed when the whole family escapes—attempts and fails to pass. When Dick Owens initially considers the idea of freeing one of his father's slaves to impress Charity, he contemplates his personal attendant, "a rather bright looking young mulatto" who comments that he would not mind going North with Dick as long as "you'd take keer er me an' fetch me home all right" (270). Tom adopts the persona of a Sambo, but this performance is not convincing: "Tom's eyes belied his words, however, and his young master felt well assured that Tom needed only a good opportunity to make him run way" (271). Colonel Owens does not, in fact, allow Tom to go north because Tom looks too "smart" (272) and the colonel even suspects him of knowing how to read: "I saw him with a newspaper the other day, and while he pretended to be looking at a woodcut, I'm almost sure he was reading the paper. I think it by no means safe to take him [north]" (272). At times Tom lets sparks of his real personality and abilities show and this limits his opportunities to obtain freedom.

Grandison, on the other hand, conceals his intelligent, resourceful personality extremely well. The Colonel comments that Grandison is too fond of "good eating" (272) and "sweet on [another slave] Betty" (272), whom he will permit Grandison to marry in the fall. Colonel Owens considers Grandison to be "abolitionist proof" (274). Grandison knows the script that he is supposed to perform:

"I should just like to know, Grandison, whether you don't think yourself a great deal better off than those poor free negroes down by the plank road, with no kind master to look after them and no mistress to give them medicine when they're sick and—and" [asks Colonel Owens].

"Well, I sh'd jes' reckon I is better off, suh, dan dem low-down free niggers, suh! Ef anybody ax 'em who dey b'long ter, dey has ter say nobody, er e'se lie erbout it. Anybody ax me who I b'longs ter, I ain't got no 'casion ter be shame' ter tell 'em, no, suh, 'deed I ain', suh!" [responds Grandison]. (272)

As Joel Taxel argues, "to the Colonel, Grandison typified the best qualities possessed by his bondsmen: humility, loyalty, and servility—a true Sambo" (108). More importantly, perhaps, from this exchange it appears that Grandison cannot even imagine a system outside of slavery, in which one might belong to one's self; hegemonic discourse dictates that one belongs to the master or to "nobody," that one is placed within the system of slavery or displaced, homeless, and ashamed of this lowly status. In another context Alfred Arteaga comments that "autocolonialism, in the extreme, requires the other's adoption of the hegemonic discourse. . . . The other assimilates both discourse and the relationships it systematizes, so to the degree the discourse suppresses, the autocolonist effaces or denigrates him/herself from within" (77). Grandison, it seems, has adopted the racist discourse of the slave system, which configures slavery as a "blissful relationship of kindly protection on the one hand, of wise subordination and loyal dependence on the other!" (Chesnutt, "Passing" 272).

Grandison's recitation has its intended result: "The colonel was beaming. This was true gratitude, and his feudal heart thrilled at this appreciative homage" (272). When Grandison is later given permission to go north with Dick and promised, upon his return, "a present, and a string of beads for Betty to wear when you and she get married in the fall" (273), he is said to be "oozing gratitude at every pore," as he intones: "Thanky, marster, thanky, marster! You is de bes' marster any nigger ever had in dis worl'" (274). Grandison's act is complete as he "bowed and scraped and disappeared round the corner" (274), but the irony of this last comment, while lost on the colonel, should not be lost on an attentive reader. Perhaps being the "best marster" any slave "ever had in dis worl'" is faint praise and calls to mind Frederick Douglass's memorable comment in his 1845 *Narrative* that William Freeland was "the best master I ever had, till I became my own master" (90). Since Chesnutt wrote a biography of Douglass that was published in 1899 (the same year *The Wife of His Youth* was published), he was certainly deliberate in placing these ironic words in Grandison's mouth.[3] This irony, however, is lost on the colonel.

The colonel's son Dick is a somewhat more dubious reader of Grandison's performance and he initially believes that Grandison will attempt to escape in the North: "For while not exactly skeptical about Grandison's perfervid loyalty, Dick had been a somewhat keen observer of human nature, in his own indolent way, and based his expectation upon the force of the example and the argument that his servant could scarcely fail to encounter" (274). Yet after Grandison repeatedly turns down abolitionist offers of freedom and even refuses to abscond with a hundred dollars that Dick tempts him with, Dick becomes convinced of the "stupidity of a slave who could be free and would not" (276). Even Dick is eventually taken in by Grandison's passing. But Dick fails to see what is obvious and parallel to his own situation. Dick is presumably madly in love with Charity, to the point that he is willing to do just about anything to gain her approval. Grandison, he knows, loves the enslaved woman Betty, yet Dick fails to even consider that this might be a partial motivation for why a slave "could be free and would not." A final point needs to be made here as well. Dick is not an abolitionist, and in general he is not committed to the liberation of his father's slaves. He is irritated enough with Grandison's behavior to register "a secret vow that if he were unable to get rid of Grandison without assassinating him, and were therefore compelled to take him back to Kentucky, he would see that Grandison got a taste of an article of slavery that would make him regret his wasted opportunities" (276); in other words, Dick plans to whip Grandison if he fails to get him to escape. Dick would not be sympathetic to Grandison's plan to escape with his whole family, so it is necessary that Grandison keep up his passing performance, even with Dick, who is allegedly trying to set him free.

Grandison's production of the role of contented, passive slave is therefore entirely successful until the end of the story, when this identity passes away forever. From the decks of a steamboat heading toward Canada, Grandison points out his former master to a crew member, who only waves his hand "derisively" toward the colonel (282). Passing, as has been noted elsewhere, is also a term that has metonymic associations with death (or passing away), and we might say here that the persona of the passive, stupid, Sambo-like slave passes away here as well. However, that would be to assume that this persona actually existed as more than a performance, when readers are nowhere led to believe that it ever did. Lorne Fienberg argues that Grandison's "own motivation and power remain invisible to the end" (219), but I would argue that this is not precisely the case. There are hints as to the real individual who lies behind the mask, beyond the story's title (which should alert us that some sort of performance is ongoing) and the double-entendres and irony of Grandison's words. Another clue to the "real" Grandison is provided by his unusual name, which Chesnutt cleverly interweaves with the history of abolition and religious debates about free will and active versus passive salvation.

Charles Grandison Finney (1792–1875) was a powerful minister who changed the face of American evangelism. In his memoirs he claims that beginning in 1821 he rejected the Calvinist doctrine of passive salvation available only to the elect; he averred that God offered Himself to everyone (Hardman 45–48). In other words, Finney argued for free will and an active approach to redemption. Finney was therefore a crucial figure of the Jacksonian era; like Andrew Jackson, Finney stressed equality of mankind, free will, and self-governance (Hardman 230). In addition to being an extremely successful and popular Christian evangelist, Finney was an abolitionist and he often denounced slavery from the pulpit in vivid terms. Furthermore, beginning in the 1830s, he controversially denied communion to slaveholders in his church (Hambrick-Stowe 142). Chesnutt's story is set in the 1850s (Hambrick-Stowe 268), when Finney's legacy was well known. It seems unlikely that a slave owner would choose such a subversive name for a slave, and more plausible to imagine that Grandison or his family picked it, hoping the colonel would not catch its dissident quality. Grandison's name seems an odd one for a passive, contented slave, since its originator stressed abolitionism, an active rather than passive approach to "salvation" (whether from slavery or religious damnation), and free will. Certainly, an attentive reader might find this parallel ironic, but she or he might not necessarily believe that Grandison's performance of the Sambo-like persona was entirely false—that is, until the last two paragraphs of the story.

When Chesnutt finally reveals that Grandison has master-minded the escape of his family unit, a trickster-like, multi-faceted individual emerges from behind the mask of the Sambo doll, leaving characters within the story, as well as the readers, profoundly destabilized in their concepts of racial identity. Perhaps the reader, like the white characters within the story, has been thinking in binarisms: Grandison is either a Sambo or a "bright mulatto" who wants to escape (like Tom); he is either servile *or* resistant. But the story shows the fallacy of such binarisms, and the reader must realize that Grandison might need to be both a Sambo *and* a cunning resister of slavery at one and the same time to attain his freedom. To understand how this binarism is first maintained and then deconstructed, however, we need to look more closely at how the story passes formally and textually.[4]

FORMAL PERFORMANCES: TEXTUAL STRATEGIES OF PASSING

On the narrative level, passing breaks down binary divisions such as appearance versus reality, "good" versus bad slave, and even master versus mastered; in the end Grandison has "mastered" the colonel, or at least rendered him "impotent" (282). But passing also functions on a textual (or generic/formal) level. Like Grandison, the text passes for something it is not. Initially, it appears to pass as a romance. The entire first section, indeed, is a false start: "When it is said that it was done to please a woman, there ought perhaps to be enough said to explain anything; for what a man will not do to please a woman has yet to be discovered" (268). By focusing on the relationship between Charity and Dick, and whether Charity will accept Dick's proposal of marriage, the first section deflects attention away from the narrative of Grandison's escape. Furthermore, the tone and point of view also distract the reader from reading the text as an indictment of slavery, making comments such as, "a young white man from Ohio, moved by compassion for the suffering of a certain bondman who happened to have a 'hard master,' essayed to help the slave to freedom" (268). The quotes around "hard master" imply that the narrator does not believe the slave's story. Even the voice of narration, then, is complicit with the story's intricate formal acts of passing; the story's opening and its point of view cover over the text's radical aims.

While the story's first section may pass as a romance, its second and third sections then pass as a plantation tradition narrative.[5] In the post–Civil War southern plantation school of writing, slavery was portrayed as a "benevolent" patriarchal institution, and slaves were depicted as happy and content. According to Amy Kaplan, the "plantation tradition" that romanticized slavery was invented by Thomas Nelson Page; Page's *In Ole Virginia* (1887) was "a collection of dialect stories narrated by a faithful ex-slave who reminisces nostalgically about 'dem good ole times'" (244). Critics have noted that Chesnutt's *The Conjure Woman* (1899) both mimics and mocks this tradition, but "The Passing of Grandison" also alludes (ironically, as we eventually see) to this school of writing.[6] In the second and third section of the text, Grandison's characterization seems to be firmly within this tradition, as he speaks entirely in dialect and "remained faithfully at his post, awaiting his master's return" (278), even though Dick has taken him to Canada, given him money, and subtly encouraged him to escape. Dick himself directly references the plantation tradition when he comments, after deciding to pay individuals to kidnap Grandison into freedom, "sleep on, faithful and affectionate servitor, and dream of the blue grass and the bright skies of old Kentucky, for it is only in your dreams that you will ever see them again!" (278). As Kenneth Warren has noted, the creation of a "happy darky" image in the post–Civil War era may have allowed whites to indulge their nostalgia for a lifestyle that was no longer available (119). Literally, no one in the United States would ever see the "happy" days depicted in the plantation school of writing again; "the old ways were beyond recovery" (119). In the post–Civil War era, Chesnutt's story at first would seem to be within this tradition of nostalgia for the old days of slavery, the days when slaves and masters together formed a "blissful relationship" (Chesnutt, "Passing" 272). But it is only passing generically for this tradition and eventually it ruthlessly undercuts it.

The final section of the story (section four) also passes, but here the genre that it passes for is inverted, as Grandison keeps his back steadily to the North and returns to his home in the South. In slave narratives, the slave sometimes follows the North Star to freedom and then is greeted (eventually) by abolitionists and sometimes reunited with his or her family. Chesnutt's text reverses this paradigm, and Grandison has a loving reunion with his "family" (that is, his master) in the South. The colonel embraces Grandison warmly, remarking that Grandison has been kept in slavery in the North: "Those infernal abolitionists are capable of anything—everything! Just think of their locking the poor, faithful nigger up, beating him, kicking him, *depriving him of his liberty*, keeping him on bread and water for three long, lonesome weeks, and he all the time pining for the old plantation" (281, emphasis added). Again, the colonel fails to notice the irony here; he complains that the abolitionists are depriving Grandison of "his liberty" when he (the colonel) quite literally keeps Grandison enslaved. In the South, Grandison is feted and celebrated: "The colonel killed the fatted calf for Grandison, and for two or three weeks the returned wanderer's life was a slave's dream of pleasure" (281). Moreover, as Grandison's fame spreads he is given a permanent place among the house servants, where the colonel "could always have him conveniently at hand to relate his adventures to admiring visitors" (281). Instead of telling the story of his escape from slavery, as many slave narrators did, Grandison tells instead the story of his return, the return of the prodigal slave.

The story, then, appears to pass for an inverted slave narrative, in which freedom and happiness are associated with the South, not the North. But such a reading is violently subverted by the story's last two paragraphs, in which it is revealed that Grandison's true goal is escape for his family. Moreover, Grandison and his family willingly turn their backs on the "freedom" of slavery: "the look they cast backward was not one of longing for the fleshpots of Egypt" (282). Unlike some of the older Jews in *Exodus*, who are said to have become accustomed to being enslaved in Egypt and long for a return to it, Grandison and his family embrace their newfound freedom. Perhaps a reader has been distracted by the many genres the text mimics and inverts: the romance tradition, the plantation school of writing, and the slave narrative. Or perhaps, as Fienberg argues, readers are "held in narrative bondage" and "shackled by the master's delusions of perfect control over their slaves' minds and motives" (219). But here the reader must finally see Chesnutt's story for what it is: a story about an intelligent enslaved individual who desires and attains liberty not just for himself, but for the family he loves. It could be argued that what this story finally most closely resembles is an actual slave narrative, but this fact is very cleverly disguised by the other genres it passes for or mimics.

READERS READING WITHIN AND OUTSIDE OF THE TEXT: THE EFFECTS OF THE PASSING PERFORMANCE

If, as I have argued elsewhere, characters who pass within texts function as "sliding signifiers" that disrupt the fixity of categories of race, gender, class, and sexuality (Cutter 95–98), it seems important to ask at this juncture what effect Grandison's passing behavior has on individuals within the text and on the reader of the text. The characterization of Grandison as Sambo-like and submissive is so effective that many contemporary readers to whom I have taught this text take the appearance as the reality (despite the story's title and the double-entendres of some of Grandison's statements).[7] They are then angered by the story's conclusion and sometimes even refuse to admit that the "real" Grandison is not the Sambo-like slave, but a clever and thoughtful individual. Yet it becomes clear that Grandison uses each of his contacts with abolitionists in the North to arrange the escape. Why do some readers resist what Chesnutt makes patent: that Grandison is not a "happy darky"?

One of the things Chesnutt is certainly writing about in this story is embedded racism and how it allows us to conveniently place individuals into categories that we believe to be fixed and absolute. And Chesnutt is also writing about the destabilization that might result if we give up these categories, if we accept the openness and instability of the system of signs that, in fact, creates race and racialized identities. Within the text, the colonel is said to have "pronounced views on the subject of negroes, having studied them, as he often said, for a great many years, and, as he asserted oftener still, understanding them perfectly" (271). The colonel also believes that he can force his slaves to abide by his system of legislated brutality and dehumanization. For example, he promises Grandison that when he returns from the North, he will be able to marry Betty, believing that Grandison will (quite conveniently) forget that any "marriage" between two slaves in the South had no legal sanction. Judging by the fact that Grandison is said at the end of the story to escape with "his wife, Betty the maid" (281), it seems that Grandison has already taken on a marital relationship with Betty, whether or not this is "sanctioned" by the colonel's system of legal justice. The colonel believes he "understands" all blacks perfectly, but the text shows him to be completely in the dark about what Grandison and the other slaves are really thinking, feeling, and doing. Grandison and his family have apparently adopted their own system of signs to construct their identities and their worlds, and this is a system about which the colonel, despite his alleged "understanding" of slaves, knows nothing.

After Grandison's escape, the colonel is said to almost lose this certainty: "About three weeks after Grandison's return the colonel's faith in sable humanity was rudely shaken, and its foundations almost broken up. He came near losing his belief in the fidelity of the negro to his master—the servile virtue most highly prized and most sedulously cultivated by the colonel and his kind" (281). This is one of the most extraordinary passages in the entire story, as it hints that the colonel's racist reading of the world and of his slaves is shaken and *almost* destroyed. The apparent gap between the signifier ("Grandison") and the signified ("cunning, intelligent, rebel") perhaps also shakes the colonel's system of signification—the way he has made meaning in his world—to its very foundation, for, indeed, this system of signification has depended on a confident "othering" of blacks as servile and subhuman to establish the authority and freedom of the white, male, slaveholding subject. The encounter with Grandison, who turns out to be a very unstable sign within the textual world of the story, has also disrupted (if not quite destroyed) the colonel's racist reading of the world, his ability to place his slaves (and all blacks, in fact) into stable categories as "good" or "bad," "contented" or "rebellious."

I would argue that a similar process takes place in a reader who reads this text and is initially tricked by its passing performance. We cannot, as Chesnutt shows us, judge a book by its cover—a theme that a story such as "Baxter's Procustes" (1904) makes abundantly clear. Someone who seems to be a "good slave" may be longing for freedom. And someone who appears to be a "good reader" may be fooled by racial ideologies and generic conventions that he or she takes for granted. Finally, texts about passing, such as this one, are designed to make us cognizant of how we get caught up in binary categories and stereotypical ideologies that limit our ability to see the complexity of any given racial or textual situation. The term "passing" has many different connotations beyond its racial one; one can be said to pass (i.e., forge) a bad check or to pass (i.e., conjure) a magic trick. And one can, of course, pass over (die). I would suggest that Chesnutt's text commits an act of forgery when it pretends to be something it is not, and an act of conjuring when it convinces us that Grandison is a contented slave, but then pulls off his mask. But in conjuring and forging, Chesnutt has powerful aims: he asks readers to *pass over* into a different way of reading and thinking about race and identity itself. Many readers end the text with a profound sense of perplexity, for like the colonel they have been fooled, tricked, and conjured; unlike the colonel, though, perhaps they have learned an important lesson. In the future perhaps these readers will read race and texts about race more carefully. And perhaps they will become more aware not just of the complexity of race itself, but of the ideologies that create racist ways of thinking. Finally, they may become more resistant readers when encountering textual and cultural systems of signs that create and reinforce restrictive ways of thinking about human identity, in all its vast complexity.

Notes

This article originally appeared in *CEA Critic* 70.2 (2008), copyright Martha J. Cutter, and is used here with permission.

1. This negative view of passing continues in some twentieth-century critical discourse; for example, Michael Cooke argues that passing is "self-assertion as self-denial, self-annihilation as self-fulfillment" (32). I would argue, instead, that passing in some situations (such as in this story) actually leads not to self-annihilation but self-fulfillment—that is, freedom. Furthermore, from a historical perspective the term "passing" has such plasticity of meaning that it can connote a whole range of behaviors and ideologies that may be complicit or subversive, enslaving or freeing, hegemonic or transgressive.

2. Other texts about passing that function in a similar manner are Mark Twain's *Puddn'head Wilson* (1894), which passes itself off at times as a light-hearted farce and other times as a detective fiction, and Jessie Fauset's *Plum Bum* (1928), which passes itself off as a romance. Fauset even subtitles *Plum Bun* "A Novel without a Moral," but clearly it has many "morals" regarding the economic, social, and cultural construction of both race and gender. See also James Weldon Johnson's *Autobiography of an Ex-Colored Man* (1912), which purported to be an autobiography but was not, so that "the form of the book constitutes in itself an act of passing" (Sollors 265).

3. Because Chesnutt's story takes place in the 1850s (268), it is possible to imagine that Grandison had read or even heard these famous words of Frederick Douglass, but the story gives us no clues on this point.

4. P. Jay Delmar argues that many of Chesnutt's stories use masking; their "ultimate meanings and denouements are often hidden from the reader, each piece working artistically through ironic or satiric structures which seek to delay the reader's perception of the last truth as long as possible" (365). Delmar also argues that Chesnutt "seldom misses a chance to delude a reader with the glimpse of a false trail" (366). Delmar does not, however, examine the significance of the trope of passing or how it functions on a narrative and textual level.

5. For other critics who have discussed how Chesnutt's story exploits the plantation school of writing, see William Andrews (93–94), Myles Hurd (83), and Sarah Meer (6–8). Meer, in particular, argues convincingly that Chesnutt, in using this genre, takes "his stand on enemy ground and revis[es] fictions which were themselves part of the problem" (5); she also discusses the story's connection to pro-slavery novels of the 1850s.

6. Kenneth Warren explains the function of this tradition: "The happy-go-lucky darky images of the antebellum South could be contrasted favorably to the images of impoverished, potentially dangerous blacks of post-Reconstruction. Such contrasts were staples of plantation fiction and minstrelsy, both of which were going strong through the 1890s" (119).

7. It should be clear that I do not agree with Delmar's statement that before the end of the story "Chesnutt never gives any indication that the slave is anything other than the Sambo he appears to be" (372). In fact, there are clues in the title of the story, in the ironic words Grandison speaks, and in Grandison's own name, but they are very subtle.

Works Cited

Andrews, William. *The Literary Career of Charles W. Chesnutt*. Baton Rouge: Louisiana State UP, 1980.

Arteaga, Alfred. *Chicano Poetics: Heterotexts and Hybridities*. New York: Cambridge UP, 1997.

Chesnutt, Charles. *Frederick Douglass*. Boston: Small, 1899.

———. "The Passing of Grandison." 1899. *Charles W. Chesnutt: Selected Writings*. Ed. SallyAnn Ferguson. Boston: Houghton, 2001. 268–282.

Cooke, Michael G. *Afro-American Literature in the Twentieth Century: The Achievement of Intimacy*. New Haven: Yale UP, 1984.

Cutter, Martha J. "Sliding Significations: Passing as a Narrative and Textual Strategy in Nella Larsen's Fiction." *Passing and the Fictions of Identity*. Ed. Elaine K. Ginsburg. Durham: Duke UP, 1996. 75–100.

Delmar, P. Jay. "The Mask as Theme and Structure: Charles Chesnutt's 'The Sheriff's Children' and 'The Passing of Grandison.'" *American Literature* 51 (1979): 364–375.

Douglass, Frederick. *Narrative of the Life of Frederick Douglass, an American Slave, Written by Himself*. 1845. New York: Penguin, 1968.

Fienberg, Lorne. "Charles W. Chesnutt's *The Wife of His Youth*: The Unveiling of the Black Storyteller." *Critical Essays on Charles Chesnutt*. Ed. Joseph R. McElrath Jr. New York: Hall, 1999. 206–223.

Hambrick-Stowe, Charles E. *Charles G. Finney and the Spirit of American Evangelicalism*. Grand Rapids: Eerdmans, 1996.

Hardman, Keith J. *Charles Grandison Finney, 1792–1875: Revivalist and Reformer*. New York: Syracuse UP, 1987.

Hildreth, Richard. *The Slave; or, Memoirs of Archy Moore*. Boston: John H. Eastburn, 1836.

Hurd, Myles Raymond. "Step by Step: Codification and Construction in Chesnutt's 'The Passing of Grandison.'" *Obsidian II* 4.3 (1989): 78–90.

Kaplan, Amy. "Nation, Region, and Empire." *Columbia History of the American Novel*. New York: Columbia UP, 1991. 240–266.

Meer, Sarah. "The Passing of Charles Chesnutt: Mining the White Tradition." *Wasafiri* 27 (1998): 5–10.

Sollors, Werner. *Neither Black nor White yet Both: Thematic Explorations of Interracial Literature.* New York: Oxford UP, 1997.

Taxel, Joe. "Charles Waddell Chesnutt's Sambo: Myth and Reality." *Negro American Literature Forum* 9 (1975): 105–108.

Warren, Kenneth. *Black and White Strangers: Race and American Literary Realism.* Chicago: U of Chicago P, 1993.

Webb, Frank. *The Garies and Their Friends.* 1857. New York: Arno, 1969.

The Dream of History
Memory and the Unconscious in Charles Chesnutt's
The House behind the Cedars

Aaron Ritzenberg

Dreams circulate throughout Charles Chesnutt's 1900 novel, *The House behind the Cedars*. Chesnutt describes the characters' lives and wishes as dreams, and an entire community reenacts dreamlike fantasies. Indeed, the novel is structured like a dream, driven by uncanny coincidences, strange doublings, and sudden shifts in time. As we trace the lives of siblings John and Rena, two light-skinned blacks who pass for white in the Deep South in the years following the Civil War, we move with the characters between black and white societies. Chesnutt's novel, even as it shows the falsity of a binary racial system, presents a distinct black consciousness and a distinct white consciousness. Passing between black and white is not only a spatial movement, but a movement between two cultures that have entirely different ways of thinking about time and history. We see that history is a function of wish fulfillments, repression, and imperfect memory, rather than an objective recollection of events. History becomes closely tied to dreams. For Chesnutt, as for Freud, we must labor to unpack the hidden meanings of dreams, for they contain the mystery of our selves, secret even to our own minds.

The exploration of history as a dream, then, becomes an investigation into the mystery of our culture. Examining what is obscured from view, what lies "behind the cedars," we see that dreams in the novel have racial coordinates. On the one hand, there is the white dream—a fantasy that culture exists outside of material history. In this waking dream, human agency and responsibility are erased; by passing off its past as organic, the white South refuses to acknowledge that its traditions have been constructed by humans interested in maintaining an oppressive power structure. On the other hand, there is the black dream that the novel associates with an entrance into the unconscious and a resolution to remember. The black dream encompasses both the literal, sleeping dream, and the American dream of social mobility. John Warwick and Rena Walden, as they pass between black and white societies, must negotiate between black and white dreams, between two opposed models of memory and history.

The opening of the book seems intentionally disorienting. Chesnutt introduces us to the world of the binary system, in which the strict distinction between black and white governs society. The author proceeds to demonstrate the utter confusion of this world when the reality of a spectrum of identity does not correspond to the binary racial model. It is not until the second chapter that we realize that John and his sister, Rena, neither of whom speak "with the dulcet negro intonation" (Chesnutt 6), are not white. William L. Andrews explains, "In a novel of passing designed to create sympathy for those whose access to social respectability is impeded only by a 'social fiction,' Chesnutt suggests the validity of their claim by passing his protagonists for white on the reader before they do so in the novel" (159). The narrator exposes our own narrative expectations and racial biases when he reveals the crucial secret. Chesnutt thematizes the root sense of the word "secret" (from *secernere*, to separate or cut); John and Rena's secret, the "secret that oppressed" (50), can cut the personal "cords of memory and affection" (8), can cleave literary expectations, and does threaten to slice violently through the fabric of a society woven with the false threads of a binary racial system that pretends to describe a universal truth.

The novel opens by positing its own ominous, universal truth: "Time touches all things with destroying hand: and if he seem now and then to bestow the bloom of youth, the sap of spring, it is but a brief mockery, to be surely and swiftly followed by the wrinkles of old age, the dry leaves and bare branches of winter" (1). The narrator seems to conceive of "Time" as an outside force that literally manipulates "all things." Human beings do not affect Time, for Time itself rules the realm of humans. We quickly realize though, that we are not in the mind of the narrator. The second paragraph begins, "Some such trite reflection—as apposite to the subject as most random reflections are—passed through the mind of a young man who came out of the front door of the Patesville Hotel about nine o'clock one fine morning in spring, a few years after the Civil War" (1). When we understand that the opening remarks about Time are not the words of the narrator, but exist inside the head of an individual, we pass from the realm of universal, cyclical time to the world of human history. Following John Warwick's mind, we move from abstraction to concreteness, from the "bloom of youth" and "wrinkles of old age" to the "front door of the Patesville Hotel." We move from a world in which humans cannot intervene with the apparently natural, unyielding progression of Time to a distinctly material human world where time is marked by a building and a clock and a war. This intellectual movement is analogous to a physical movement; following John Warwick's body, we move from a world in which John Warwick is white—his newly acquired plantation home in Clarence, South

Carolina—to reenter the world in which he is black, the small town of Patesville, North Carolina, where he was born with the name John Walden. History, especially when we conceive of it as the "destroying hand" of an all-powerful force, is actually the "trite reflection" of an individual who, at least while he makes the reflection, conceives of himself as white.

For Chesnutt, this dreamlike sense of natural history is the white fantasy that dominates Southern society. A sense of history as the natural progression of an unrelentingly destructive force defuses any attempt to change society. Social injustice rendered in natural terms resonates with the 1896 *Plessy vs. Ferguson* decision, in which the court ruled that Plessy, a light-skinned African American man who was seven-eighths white, was legally black and could be forced to sit in the separate but equal "colored" car of an East Louisiana Railroad train. As Gregg D. Crane explains:

In the Court's view, the constraint of the Constitution by tradition is inevitable: in "the nature of things" the Fourteenth Amendment "could not have been intended to abolish distinctions based upon color." By figuring tradition as nature, the Court not only exhibits the historic need of mainstream American culture to imagine law as organic and innate and to represent its edicts and ruling in the emotionally resonant language of the higher law tradition, but it also evokes an appeal to the contemporary social Darwinist image of a slowly evolving social order. (196)

The ruling culture of the South envisioned its society as reflecting universal truth. The white fantasy is that its culture adheres to the natural order of things.

As Judge Straight (Warwick's white mentor in Patesville) warns Warwick when they meet for the first time in ten years, "I wouldn't stay too long. The people of a small town are inquisitive about strangers, and some of them have long memories. I remember we went over the law, which was in your favor; but custom is stronger than law—in these matters custom *is* law" (23). The Judge uses the word "law" to mean two different things. First, he refers to the law as the set of legal agreements produced by elected officials and overseen by the courts; this law favors John Warwick. But the law in the phrase "custom *is* law" does not refer to legalities, but to natural law. This law, as a function of nature, cannot be tampered with. Natural law trumps legal law; natural law, the Judge explains, does not favor John Warwick. The Judge continues, "We make our customs lightly; once made, like our sins, they grip us in bands of steel; we become the creatures of our creations" (24). The Judge's vocabulary—"sins," "creatures," "creations"— implies that the Patesville customs are like religious, organic truth. Even while the Judge is aware of Patesville's arbitrarily despotic rule, he implicates himself in the culture. The Judge, though able to maintain some critical distance from his culture, is both a creator and a creation of Southern custom. Like a prophet describing the fury of an arbitrary god, he is at once admonitory and helpless.

John Warwick, like the Judge, is able to witness society from a privileged point of view. Inhabiting the liminal space between black and white, Warwick seems able to view Patesville from two perspectives. Upon first returning to Patesville, his "trite reflection" about the undeniable procession of Time displays his apparent adherence to the white rule of social Darwinism. When he walks down the street, "he [sees] little that [is] not familiar, or that he [has] not seen in his dreams a hundred times during the past ten years" (2). Passage back into a world where Warwick is black marks his reentrance into the world of dreams. Patesville, like a dream, is simultaneously familiar and distant. Ironically, what John recognizes from a dream is actually the concrete, material world of his hometown. Defining the actual material world as the world of dreams denies the dreamlike quality of the white perspective. The culture that professes natural law is blind to its own fantasy when it recognizes the world of objects and matter as a dream.

Chesnutt offers two competing kinds of dreams: on the one hand, there is the dreamlike fantasy, associated with whiteness, that culture adheres to natural law; on the other hand, there is the literal, unconscious dream that is associated with blackness.[1] Biracial John Warwick passes between the two kinds of dreams. Warwick notices that "here and there blackened and dismantled walls marked the place where handsome buildings once had stood, for Sherman's march to the sea had left its mark upon the town" (2). Even when Warwick seems to be stepping outside of the white dream of natural time, even when he notices the material reality of a historical moment, his observations display the seemingly indelible mark of white culture. Warwick remembers that Sherman's march wreaked much property damage, but not that the march freed and dislocated thousands of ex-slaves. Warwick's reflections relegate a black historical consciousness to the unseen and unheard.

However, Warwick has not forgotten the horrific, racist past of Patesville. Oscillating between white and black consciousnesses, he sees that

the tall tower, with its four-faced clock, rose as majestically and uncompromisingly as though the land had never been subjugated. Was it so irreconcilable, Warwick wondered, as still to peal out the curfew bell, which at nine o'clock at night had clamorously warned all negroes, slave or free, that it was unlawful for them to be abroad after that hour, under penalty of imprisonment or whipping? (2)

Warwick makes these observations at "about nine o'clock one fine morning" (1). Nine o'clock no longer signals the toll of an oppressive culture, but, as if indicating a new dawn after a historic curfew, marks a time during which a man can reflect on the tragedies and injustices of a historical moment. As William L. Andrews states, "The introduction of Patesville's monuments, which in Warwick's eyes weigh heavily, not nostalgically, on the South's moral slate, works well to Chesnutt's larger thematic purpose" (158). Indeed, the memory of the clock is the memory of humiliation and horror, a reminder of historical trauma. The clock becomes a haunting relic of subjugation and oppression. The clock tower, though, still "rose as majestically and uncompromisingly as though the land had never been subjugated." In this description, the clock represents Southern pride and resilience. The clock tower, the manifestation of Patesville's sense of time and history, still stands as if Sherman's march had never occurred, as if the Civil War were not a reality. The dominant sense of relentless, indestructible time still hovers over the land.

As a member of both the white world and the black world, Warwick has a split sense of history that appears in his observations of the clock tower. History, when symbolized by the clock that stands unblemished even after military defeat, remains unyielding and noble; whereas history, when symbolized by the clock whose bell no longer rings for oppression, is a document of social injustice. Warwick remembers his days as a black youth, when time was carefully managed by white society and the curfew bell ruled lives. Even after the curfew bell no longer rings, time continues to be ruled by the white paradigm. The clock, in the style of the Southern fantasy, stands above the historical wreckage of the Civil War.

There is a catastrophic social danger in forgetting the Civil War as a specific historical event; in his study of Civil War memory, David Blight explains, "We sometimes lift ourselves out of historical time, above the details, and render the war safe in a kind of national Passover offering as we view a photograph of the Blue and Gray veterans shaking hands across the stone walls at Gettysburg" (4). Viewed through an ahistorical lens, the Civil War becomes a reconcilable fraternal feud, whose memory symbolizes not a deep, critical wound in American society, but the sentimental union of North and South. Warwick begins the novel lifted "out of historical time, above the details." As we follow Warwick's pass-over, from white to black, we descend from abstract time to concrete history. But as the clock tower reminds us, we never fully depart from historical abstraction; and concrete history turns out not to be very solid.

As we move into detail, away from the safety of historical distance, we descend into a world of confusion and secrecy. Again Warwick's split consciousness adheres to Blight's model of Civil War memory. Blight writes,

The memory of slavery, emancipation, and the Fourteenth and Fifteenth Amendments never fit well into a developing narrative in which the Old and New South were romanticized and welcomed back to a new nationalism, and in which devotion alone made everyone right, and no one truly wrong, in the remembered Civil War. (4)

Straddling two worlds, Warwick is caught between two narratives—one that continues to remember the wounds of the Civil War era and one that attempts to seal the fractures of Southern society. When Warwick returns home after ten years of passing for white, he signals the collision of two worlds, two models of time and memory, and begins a series of events that, according to the narrative, can only end in tragedy.

Warwick's homecoming is at first an incredible blessing for his mother, Molly, and sister, Rena, for "he represented to them the world from which circumstances had shut them out, and to which distance lent even more than its usual enchantment" (13–14). Born on the dark side of a binary system, Molly and Rena believe that the life of opportunity, the life of whiteness, is forever inaccessible. When Warwick suggests taking Rena back with him into the world of passing, Molly vehemently refuses, crying, "Don't take her away from me!" (16). John argues, "Of course she will have no chance here, where our story is known. The war has wrought great changes, has put the bottom rail on top, and all that—but it hasn't wiped *that* out. Nothing but death can remove that stain, if it does not follow us even beyond the grave. Here she must forever be—nobody!" (17). "*That*" is unspeakable; "*that*" is blackness. Racial consciousness lies at the heart of Warwick's concern, but, speaking from the white perspective, blackness remains the unutterable "stain." To be black is forever to be hidden in "the house behind the cedars," to "forever be nobody."

Warwick continues to appeal to Molly, stating, "But of course it is impossible—a mere idle dream" (18).[2] Access to the dream, for Warwick, is access to whiteness. Finally Molly concedes; accepting that Rena can no longer associate with her, Molly grants her daughter the promise of America. Before Rena departs for South Carolina, the narrator explains, "All sorts of vague dreams had floated through her mind during the last few hours, as to what the future might bring forth" (27). The future holds a dream, but not just the dream of opportunity; rather, Rena will be sucked into the world of white fantasy.

The first chapter that describes John and Rena's new life, entitled "The Tournament," is central to Chesnutt's vision of Southern society. The townspeople of Clarence have gathered for their annual reenactment of a medieval contest. Chesnutt writes:

The influence of Walter Scott was strong upon the South. The South before the war was essentially feudal, and Scott's novels of chivalry appealed forcefully to the feudal heart. . . . During the month preceding the Clarence tournament, the local bookseller had closed out his entire stock of "Ivanhoe," consisting of five copies, and had taken orders for seven copies more. The tournament scene in this popular novel furnished the model after which these bloodless imitations of the ancient passages-at-arms were conducted, with such variations as were required to adapt them to a different age and civilization. (31)

The people of Clarence engage in a collective fantasy, a community-wide dream that endeavors to reenact events from Sir Walter Scott's 1791 novel, itself a story set in the twelfth century during the third crusade. The tournament is a fictional copy of a fictional copy. Chesnutt touches on an element of Southern culture that Mark Twain described two decades earlier; in his 1883 *Life on the Mississippi,* Twain writes:

the genuine and wholesome civilization of the nineteenth century is curiously confused and commingled with the Walter Scott Middle-Age sham civilization; and so you have practical, common-sense, progressive ideas, and progressive works; mixed up with the duel, the inflated speech, and the jejune romanticism of an absurd past that is dead, and out of charity ought to be buried. (304)

The society that Twain describes is a ridiculous pastiche of incongruous elements from a made-up civilization, an unwittingly ludicrous resurrection of a falsified history. The Clarence tournament, adhering to Twain's description, is doubly false; the tournament not only is a falsification of Southern society, but is based on a feudal model that is itself a fantasy.

The Tournament has the features of a Freudian dream. Freud, whose *The Interpretation of Dreams* was published in November 1899, months before Chesnutt published *The House behind the Cedars,* explains that the dream "is a fully valid psychical phenomenon, in fact a wish-fulfillment; it is to be included in the series of intelligible psychical acts of our waking life; it has been constructed by a highly elaborate intellectual activity" (98). The Tournament is the waking version of a Freudian dream; the annual event is a communal wish-fulfillment for a culture of nobility and honor, for, as Warwick explains, "the renaissance of chivalry" (32). Chesnutt writes, "The knights, masquerading in fanciful costumes, in which bright-coloured garments, gilt paper, and cardboard took the place of knightly harness, were mounted on spirited horses" (31). The artifice is apparent—ceremonial paper and cardboard replications substitute for military costume. But as Freud explains the phenomenon of "condensation" in his chapter on "The Dream Work," "the dream is scant, paltry, laconic in comparison to the range and abundance of the dream-thoughts" (212). The manifest content of the dream is only the tip of the psychical iceberg. The Tournament, as a fantasy, represents far more than a paltry reenactment for the sake of a single day's entertainment. The latent content of the Southern dream is the wish-fulfillment not only for a culture of honor, love and beauty, nobility and chivalry, but for a society whose traditions stand outside of history, whose true identity hovers above and beyond the materiality of its surroundings.

Chesnutt's fiction is the Freudian version of Twain's analysis of the South. In other words, viewed through a Freudian lens, *The House behind the Cedars* reveals the same culture that Twain indicts in *Life on the Mississippi*. Besides showing us the absurdity of the Southern dream of a Sir Walter Scott sensibility, Twain also explains the danger of a culture whose ideals rest on the *Ivanhoe* ethos. Twain writes:

Then comes Sir Walter Scott with his enchantments, and by his single might checks this wave of progress, and even turns it back; sets the world in love with dreams and phantoms; with decayed and swinish forms of religion; with decayed and degraded systems of government; with the silliness and emptinesses, sham grandeurs, sham gauds, and sham chivalries of a brainless and worthless long-vanished society. He did measureless harm; more real and lasting harm, perhaps, than any other individual that ever wrote. (303–304)

Chesnutt's characters fit perfectly into Twain's condemnation. Indeed, when Warwick shows his love for the "sham" effects of the Tournament, we know that he thinks of himself as white. Watching the event, he excitedly explains to a skeptical white woman:

Our knights are not weighted down with heavy armor, but much more appropriately attired, for a day like this, in costumes that recall the picturesqueness, without the discomfort, of the knightly harness. . . . It is a South Carolina renaissance which has points of advantage over the tournaments of the olden time. (32)

The Tournament for Warwick, in its nonadherence to historical detail (detail that is dubious in the first place), is a cultural victory, an improvement upon past societies. Once again Warwick speaks from a viewpoint that imagines itself outside the realm of historical time.

The most insidious aspect of the Tournament is not the manifest masquerade, but that the masquerade, in its latent form, persists once the Tournament is over. As Freud would interpret the Tournament as a dream, the ideals embodied in the Tournament are merely the manifest forms of latent Southern desires. A Freudian analysis of Chesnutt's fiction reveals what Twain saw clearly when he argued that Sir Walter Scott's pernicious influence lies deeper than the mere surface effects of preposterous masquerades. Twain explains, "For it was he that created rank and caste down there, and also reverence for rank and caste, and pride and pleasure in them. Enough is laid on slavery, without fathering upon it these creations and contributions of Sir Walter" (304). Indeed, rank and caste are an important, almost unnoticed part of the Tournament. The narrator explains that the "best people gradually filled the grand stand, while the poorer white and colored folks found seats outside, upon what would now be known as the 'bleachers,' or stood alongside the lists" (31). The Tournament, indeed, is a celebration of "rank and caste"; the use of Sir Walter Scott becomes the high culture justification that rank and caste are somehow critical to the vitality of a genteel society.

In his most scathing attack of the *Ivanhoe* legacy, Twain senses an undercurrent of violence and tragedy in the Walter Scott inheritance. Twain writes, "Sir Walter had so large a hand in making Southern character, as it existed before the war, that he is in great measure responsible for the war" (304). For Twain, it is nearly impossible to overestimate the role of the South's medieval fantasy in determining the very fate and character of the country. Similarly, the unconscious drives behind the Tournament hold the psychological key to Chesnutt's nightmarish depiction of the South. As in Twain's vision, there is a layer of actual violence in the Clarence recreation. The new Tournament purports to be safe; Warwick proudly declares, "If our knights do not run the physical risks of Ashby-de-la-Zouch, they have all the mental stimulus. Wounded vanity will take the place of wounded limbs, and there will be broken hopes in lieu of broken heads" (33). The competitors substitute games of athletic skill for actual jousts and sword fighting; none of them get physically hurt. There is, though, one broken head. A horse reared and broke a lance,

and sent a broken piece of it flying over the railing opposite the grand stand, into the middle of a group of spectators standing there. The flying fragment was dodged by those who saw it coming, but brought up with a resounding thwack against the head of a colored man in the second row, who stood watching the grand stand with an eager and curious gaze. He rubbed his head ruefully, and made a good-natured response to the chaffing of his neighbors, who, seeing no great harm done, made witty and original remarks about the advantage of being black upon occasions where one's skull was exposed to danger. (33)

The incidental victim of the Tournament is an unnamed black man. The fact that we find out fifty pages later that the man is Frank, Rena's only "loyal friend" (84), underscores the anonymity of his victimization when he is hurt. Frank is, as John feared Rena would remain, a black "nobody." Indeed, the anonymous injured black man becomes an impromptu part of the entertainment. Even though "the blow had drawn blood" (33), the man, in the eyes of the audience, seems not to be truly hurt. The white fantasy is not entirely blind to its black victims, but the black casualty is merely incidental, a slightly entertaining side note to the central fantasy. An injured black man is certainly no threat to break the spell of the day's entertainment.

Rena, no longer a "nobody," is suddenly a full participant in the Tournament events. She accidentally drops her handkerchief, which in true Romance fashion is caught by the eventual victor "on the point of his lance ere it touched the ground" (34). "Sir George," upon his victory in the Tournament, chooses "Miss Rowena Warwick" as the "Queen of Love and Beauty" (37). With the help of a dropped garment and an eager lance Rena is suddenly thrust into the center of the white fantasy.

At the close of the evening, Warwick tells his sister, "Now that the masquerade is over, let us to sleep, and to-morrow take up the serious business of life" (42). For Warwick the Tournament fantasy is a distinct moment, an enjoyable break from "the serious business of life." The masquerade instills the belief that there is, in fact, an authentic, stable identity underneath the mask, that life beyond the Tournament is not a masquerade. About to fall asleep, Rena concurs with Warwick, declaring, "It is a dream . . . only a dream. I am Cinderella before the clock has struck" (42). Rena recognizes the fantasy as her own dream, not realizing that the Tournament is, in fact, the dream of an entire culture. The description of herself as Cinderella is unwittingly astute.

Like Cinderella at the end of the magical evening, Rena will no longer be the "Queen of Love and Beauty"; but also like Cinderella, the end of the ball does not signal the end of the fantasy. Even when no longer clad in the gown, Rena has been irrevocably changed once she has entered the dream of the South. The fantasy has a real effect on Rena. Tryon "had crowned her Queen of Love and Beauty; since then she had ascended the throne of his heart. He would make her queen of his home and mistress of his life" (48). Tryon cannot help but use the vocabulary of the Tournament when he describes his most interior emotions. He is a full product of the Southern dream. Rena, too, has imbibed the South's fantasy. When she returns home in the second half of the novel, she is fundamentally different. The narrator explains, "If Frank felt the difference in her attitude, he ascribed it to the fact that she had been white, and had taken on something of the white attitude toward the Negro; and Frank, with an equal unconsciousness, clothed her with the attributes of the superior race" (87). Merely passing as white, masquerading as the defined other, has deep unconscious effects on Rena's identity.

After the Tournament, Rena falls in love with the knight who crowned her, but worries that her secret will cut the cords of her fantasy. Warwick gives his sister advice: "Marriage is a reciprocal arrangement, by which the contracting parties give love for love, care for keeping, faith for faith. It is a matter of the future, not of the past" (54). Intermingling the words of law and religion, Warwick echoes Judge Straight's vocabulary: marriage is a contract of faith. In Warwick's eyes, there is an element of religious truth to the law, which looks forward to a future of redemption. Warwick continues in religious terms:

What a poor soul it is that has not some secret chamber, sacred to itself; where one can file away the things others have no right to know, as well as things that one himself would fain forget! We are under no moral obligation to inflict upon others the history of our past mistakes, our wayward thoughts, our secret sins, our desperate hopes, or our heart-breaking disappointments. (54)

Warwick offers a list of what ought to be forgotten, referring to only one thing: the unspeakable "stain" of blackness. In his passing, Warwick seems to have fully absorbed the culture of whiteness. There is an element of self-contempt in his words, as he describes his own longing to forget his earlier ascribed identity. His language assigns blame not to society, but to those not born into society's power. As if racial impurity is an inherent character flaw, blackness becomes a function of "our past mistakes." For Warwick, as for the South, the envisioned future cannot exist with a fully remembered past.

To succeed in Southern society, to abide by contractual and religious law, is to erase that which does not adhere to a vision of binary truth. History must be carefully screened, so that challenges to governing notions of truth are pushed beneath the surface, locked in a "secret chamber." To use the language of Freud, a history *of* repression *is* repression. As Blight tells us, the fraught memory of the Civil War in the United States has been dominated by communal repression to allow for a "reconciliationist vision" (389). In a culture of willed amnesia, "a homegrown beneficent Fate governed American memory. Such a depoliticized memory, cleansed of any lessons about the war's unresolved legacy of racial strife, had indeed fostered reconciliation among soldiers, politicians, businessmen, and scholars. But sectional peace had its costs" (Blight 389). Indeed, Gettysburg Veterans from the North and the South have shaken hands, but segregation, lynching, and Jim Crow laws lasted for generations. Blight continues, "monuments and reunions had always combined remembrance with healing and, therefore, with forgetting" (389). As Warwick suggests, the way to heal Rena's emotional pain is by forgetting her past. For Rena to remain in the Southern dream, which has become her own heart-wrenchingly emotional fantasy, she must forget.

After some deliberation, Rena consciously decides to alter her memory. She "was willing to bury the past in forgetfulness, now that she knew it would have no interest for her lover" (59). Rena's indulgence in her new fantasy, though, does not last long before it is interrupted by another dream. Worriedly, she explains to her brother, "I dreamed last night that mother was ill" (61). Warwick simply replies, "Dreams . . . go by contraries. Yours undoubtedly signifies that our mother, G-d bless her simple soul! is at the present moment enjoying her usual perfect health" (61). Warwick seems to be offering his own Freudian interpretation of the dream. Indeed, Freud, defining "displacement," explains that "what is clearly essential in the content of the dream-thoughts does not need to be represented in the dream itself at all" (232). But Rena continues to be disturbed by dreams. Chesnutt, too, seems disturbed by dreams, as the narrator wonders about their significance and interpretation for some length. As if anticipating Freud's obsession, Chesnutt writes, "Science, which has shattered many an idol and destroyed many a delusion, has made but slight inroads upon the shadowy realm of dreams" (62). Dreams are eminently mysterious, but for Warwick and Molly Walden, "a dream three times repeated was a certain portent of the thing defined" (62). Rena's third dream of her ill mother, then, arrives "with the force of a fateful warning and a great reproach" (63). Soon after Rena's third dream, Molly writes a letter that "confirm[s] the warning" of Rena's dream (64). When Rena decides that she must return to Patesville, the tone of the novel shifts. If the first half of the novel documents the rise of Rena in white society, the second half of the novel charts her precipitous decline and death once she has returned to black society.

The two versions of the dream that lay behind Warwick's early observations of Patesville have collided. The unconscious dream associated with Rena's blackness punctures the waking fantasy associated with her whiteness; the repressed returns as the oppressed emerges. In the novel, dreams reflect conditions outside of the body just as they affect the body itself. When Molly begins to understand her daughter's misfortune, she laments that "if she had not been sick, Rena would not have dreamed the fateful dream that had brought her to Patesville" (132). Molly and, indeed, the novel itself acknowledge the real effects of dreams on individuals. But the novel treats the waking fantasy differently than it does the unconscious nocturnal vision. Indeed, by having a sleeping dream interrupt the living dream of the Southern fantasy, the novel obfuscates the dream quality of Rena's waking life in white society.

The waking fantasy of white society, though, adheres more to Freud's version of the dream than do the literal dreams of the novel. The central sleeping vision in the novel, when Rena dreams that her mother is ill, has manifest content that, in an un-Freudian way, matches its latent meaning. However, the waking dreams of the first half of the novel, in a Freudian way, are an extended wish-fulfillment, a depiction of a white society that exists above materiality, outside of historical time. The second half of the novel, too, seems a product of unconscious desires, a waking dream.

The plot of Rena's swift decline rests on a chain of unlikely coincidences that include sudden implausible encounters, unread letters, an envelope blown by the wind, a downed tree that causes a critical detour, and extended sequences of improbable timing. P. Jay Delmar declares, "Chesnutt used coincidence to emphasize the role played by forces external to the characters in the downfall of the characters themselves, thus creating a nearly tragic action without the necessity of stressing any weaknesses within his protagonists" (97). More importantly, though, Chesnutt uses coincidence because its uncanniness is one of the hallmarks of the dream.

The coincidences lead to a single major revelation—George Tryon finds out that Rena is not white. The Cinderella fantasy fully collapses as Tryon reveals the raving racist behind the Prince Charming mask. Tryon's "love and yearning had given place to anger and disgust" (95). The narrator explains that "Tryon's liberality, of which he had spoken so nobly and so sincerely, had been confined unconsciously, and as a matter of course, within the boundaries of his own race" (96). Tryon's unconscious, his deepest self, is fundamentally racist. Indeed, in Tryon's dream, Rena turns from a "fair young beauty" into "a hideous black hag" whose "beautiful tresses become mere wisps of coarse wool," whose "clear eyes grow bloodshot," and whose "ivory teeth turn to unwholesome fangs" (98). On an unconscious level, Tryon can only see Rena through the most virulently racist lens.

What lies at the very center of the white fantasy is the belief that identity can be reduced to a binary code. Tryon is sincerely troubled and shaken, and seems to question the racial system that rules his life, noticing that "even his mother, a woman of keen discernment and delicate intuitions, had been deceived by this girl's specious exterior" (168). Tryon acknowledges that skin color does not match interiority; the premise of racism is flawed. But rather than question the system, Tryon punishes the woman who has demonstrated the system's failures: "Well, he had imagined her just as pure and fine, and she had deliberately, with a negro's low cunning, deceived him into believing that she was a white girl" (168). Even as he recognizes that race does not match identity, even as he realizes the undeniable falsity of binary identification, Tryon perpetuates the central myth of the South. He will not marry Rena. Soon, though, Tryon is torn—caught between his hatred of a race and his love of a woman.[3] Despite his conscious considerations, Tyron decides to pursue Rena, declaring, "Custom was tyranny. Love was the only law" (194). Tryon offers a skewed echo of Judge Straight; but even as he revises the Judge's declaration that "custom *is* law" (23), he is himself gripped in "bands of steel" (24) and cannot overcome custom. Custom, it seems, is tyrannical not just for the oppressed, but for the oppressor. The narrative ends in tragedy not only for Rena, but for Tryon too. Just as the dream associated with Rena's blackness (the dream of her mother's illness) destroyed her white dream of high society, so does Tryon's deep, impermissible desire for a black woman rip apart his white fantasy of an orderly world of racial division.

Chesnutt, like Tryon, acknowledges the Southern fantasy as a dream; we must question whether the author, like Tryon, participates in the proliferation of the very structure he describes as false. After all, Warwick and Rena are punished when they unveil the limits of the foundational binary system of the South. In *The House behind the Cedars*, those who challenge the fundamental structure of the racist South disappear from the text. Warwick vanishes from the plot, passing back into white culture and oblivion; Rena dies. Perhaps Chesnutt, like Warwick, has absorbed the culture of the South even as he exposes its flawed inner workings.[4] Just as Freud used his own dreams as examples in *The Interpretation of Dreams,* we must wonder if Chesnutt writes personal unconscious wish-fulfillments into his own interpretation of dreams.[5]

According to the editors of his *Essays and Speeches*, Charles Chesnutt symbolized "what it meant not only to live literally on the color line but to be able to cross freely between the two camps as though that line did not exist" (McElrath xxiv). Like his creation, Warwick, Chesnutt inhabited a liminal space. Charles Duncan explains:

As a light-skinned, gray-eyed black man whose grandfather was white, Chesnutt understandably lacked a fixed or definite position from which to view racial interaction, and this ambiguity about his own racial makeup clearly affected his writings. (11)

Chesnutt lived partly within white culture, partly without; he had enough familiarity with the society to accurately portray its psyche, enough distance from the culture to critically evaluate its inherent, horrible flaws. Chesnutt, as if an anthropologist, was a participant-observer.

Like Freud, Chesnutt engaged in a critical examination of his own self. As Ritchie Robertson describes the legacy of Freud's work, "we have learnt to apply to ourselves the distant, half-perplexed gaze which an anthropologist turns on another culture" (xxxvi). Freud wondered about the accuracy of interpreting a dream which is only partly recalled. He writes, "Everything suggests that our memory not only reproduces the dream incompletely and inaccurately, but also falsifies it" (333). Our minds leave us blind to our own dreams, unable to fully perceive our own fantasies, yet the dream-work can continue. Freud explains that "this distortion is itself nothing but a part of the revision which the dream-thoughts regularly undergo as a consequence of the censorship" (334). The memory of the dream, even if it is not a complete account, *is* the dream that must be interpreted. Freud continues, "Forgetting dreams, too, will remain inexplicable unless we also include the power of the psychical censorship in our explanation of it" (336). Chesnutt, critically, remembers "the power of psychical censorship" in his examination of post–Civil War culture. In writing the white fantasy, Chesnutt charts a dream that does not realize that it is a dream, one that is fundamentally concerned with forgetting the material history of its own surroundings.

Before he passes into white culture and disappears, Warwick's final words are directed to Frank Fowler, Rena's loyal friend and the one who truly loved her: "We value your friendship, Frank, and we'll not forget it" (124). Warwick's last sentence is an insistence on memory in the face of a culture that thrives on forgetting. Frank, the anonymously injured black victim of the white fantasy, will not be forgotten. In this way, Warwick will resist white society even as he passes back into it. As Blight reminds us of our history, "Racial legacies, conflict itself, the bitter consequences of Reconstruction's failure to make good on the promises of emancipation, and the war as America's second revolution in the meaning of liberty and equality had been *seared clean* from the nation's master narrative" (391). As Chesnutt has demonstrated, the dominant history of the South is a Freudian dream, a wish-fulfillment marked by repression, displacement, and forgetting. Tryon, the voice of white culture, explains, "As slaves, negroes were tolerable. As freemen, they were an excrescence, an alien element incapable of absorption into the body politic of white men" (169). Tryon echoes and opposes Frederick Douglass, who in an 1863 speech declared that the work of the Civil War "will not be done until the colored man is admitted a full member in good and regular standing in the American body politic" (381). The critical edge to *The House behind the Cedars*, Chesnutt's act of resistance, is to continue the work of the Civil War, to show that Warwick can and will be absorbed, once again, into "the body politic of white men." This time, Warwick promises with his last words, he will remember his past.

Notes

1. In *Surface and Depth: The Quest for Legibility in American Literature*, Michael T. Gilmore notes that in works such as Ralph Ellison's *Invisible Man* and Mark Twain's *Pudd'nhead Wilson* blackness is associated with instinct and unconscious desires. He writes, "Blackness comes to be linked with unfathomable complexity and depth" (170).

2. Almost a century later, Martin Luther King Jr. would use the word "dream" in a similar sense, declaring, "I say to you today, my friends, that in spite of the difficulties and frustrations of the moment I still have a dream. It is a dream deeply rooted in the American dream" (King 605). Dream here signifies a hopeful ache, a deep longing that is not quite the stuff of reality, but lies, like a sleeping vision, on the edge of consciousness and possibility. Martin Luther

King Jr. identifies this dream as profoundly "American"; John Warwick identifies this dream as fundamentally white.

3. Matthew Wilson describes Tryon's dilemma as a struggle between "racist rationality" and "sentiment" (78). Wilson's description of Tyron's internal struggle is helpful, but the term "racist rationality" ascribes a logic to Tryon's racism that hinders us from seeing the racism as an essential element of the Southern white fantasy. At the foundation of the white fantasy is the very opposite of logic—an irrational belief in racial order so deeply rooted that it does not recognize itself as a dream.

4. Several critics have noted Chesnutt's ambivalence with regard to racial identification. See especially John Sheehy's "The Mirror and the Veil: The Passing Novel and the Quest for American Racial Identity" and Anne Fleischmann's "Neither Fish, Flesh, nor Fowl: Race and Region in the Writings of Charles W. Chesnutt."

5. SallyAnn H. Ferguson charges that "in his quest to bring racial peace and a taste of the good life to the light-skinned segment of the black population, [Chesnutt] did not hesitate to sacrifice the interests of dark-skinned people" (118).

WORKS CITED

Andrews, William L. *The Literary Career of Charles W. Chesnutt*. Baton Rouge: Louisiana State UP, 1980.

Blight, David W. *Race and Reunion: The Civil War in American Memory*. Cambridge, MA: Belknap, 2001.

Chesnutt, Charles W. *The House behind the Cedars*. 1900. New York: Penguin, 1993.

Crane, Gregg D. *Race, Citizenship, and Law in American Literature*. New York: Cambridge UP, 2002.

Delmar, P. Jay. "Coincidence in Charles W. Chesnutt's *The House behind the Cedars*." *American Literary Realism 1870–1910* 15.1 (1982): 97–103.

Douglass, Frederick. "Our Work Is Not Done." Speech Delivered at the Annual Meeting of the American Anti-Slavery Society Held at Philadelphia, December 3–4, 1863. *The Life and Writings of Frederick Douglass*, Volume 3. Ed. Philip S. Foner. New York: International, 1975.

Duncan, Charles. *The Absent Man: The Narrative Craft of Charles W. Chesnutt*. Athens: Ohio UP, 1998.

Ferguson, SallyAnn H. "Chesnutt's Genuine Blacks and Future Americans." *MELUS* 15.3 (1988): 109–119.

Fleischmann, Anne. "Neither Fish, Flesh, nor Fowl: Race and Region in the Writings of Charles W. Chesnutt." *African American Review* 34.3 (2000): 461–472.

Freud, Sigmund. *The Interpretation of Dreams*. Trans. Joyce Crick. 1899. New York: Oxford UP, 1999.

Gilmore, Michael T. *Surface and Depth: The Quest for Legibility in American Literature*. New York: Oxford UP, 2003.

King, Martin Luther, Jr. "I Have a Dream." 1963. *The Bedford Reader*. Ed. X. J. Kennedy et al. Boston: Bedford, 2003.

McElrath, Joseph R., Jr., Robert C. Leitz III, and Jesse Crisler, eds. and intro. *Charles W. Chesnutt: Essays and Speeches*. Stanford: Stanford UP, 1999. xxiii–xxxvii.

Robertson, Ritchie. Introduction. *The Interpretation of Dreams*. By Sigmund Freud. New York: Oxford UP, 1999. vii–xxxvii.

Sheehy, John. "The Mirror and the Veil: The Passing Novel and the Quest for American Racial Identity." *African American Review* 33.3 (1999): 401–415.

Twain, Mark. *Life on the Mississippi*. 1883. New York: Oxford UP, 1990.

Wilson, Matthew. *Whiteness in the Novels of Charles W. Chesnutt*. Jackson: UP of Mississippi, 2004.

In the Wake of D. W. Griffith's *The Birth of a Nation*
Chesnutt's Paul Marchand, F.M.C. *as Command Performance*

SUSAN PROTHRO WRIGHT

This essay sets forth the hypothesis that Charles Chesnutt attempted to publish his novel *Paul Marchand, F.M.C.* in 1921, with goal of countering D. W. Griffith's *The Birth of a Nation* (1915), the incendiary film version of Thomas Dixon's equally racist novel, *The Clansman* (1905), a depiction of the Reconstruction South. Substantiating this hypothesis is relevant to Chesnutt scholarship in general as well as to the further exploration of *Paul Marchand, F.M.C.*: not only does it help to answer questions about Chesnutt's decision to submit a novel for publication so long after the publication of his final ill-fated novel, *The Colonel's Dream,* in 1905, but it also reveals the novel's potential as a feasible challenge to *Birth*'s depictions of both white and black characters. In relation to this point, it is important to note that Chesnutt's political and literary activities parallel African American activism during the racially turbulent political climate from 1906 until 1921, the year Chesnutt submitted *Paul Marchand* for publication.

Looking at particular efforts and concerns of Chesnutt during this time helps to confirm his intentions for his novel. One must keep in mind that Chesnutt's strivings for his race were circumscribed by his early resolution to foment a "moral revolution" in the United States through his writing,[1] and doing so allows one to surmise that the social and legal inequities suffered by African Americans during this period were likely the prime motivator for his returning to novel writing, the genre he hoped would reverse the tide of continued discrimination against blacks in the United States. Chesnutt's role in the race struggle at the turn of the nineteenth century is, then, most obviously linked to one of the driving forces uniting African Americans in a common cause—Thomas Dixon's racist novels. Dixon's novel *The Leopard's Spots: A Romance of the White Man's Burden* (1902), later adapted for stage, was a romanticized version of the 1898 Wilmington, North Carolina, "race" riot: it blamed the friction largely on the city's black population and highlighted the need for white males to protect white females from black sexual aggression. A few years later, stage productions of the work broadened its popularity by widening its audience, serving, perhaps, as a harbinger of the racial discord of the period. As Patrick Gerster and Nicholas Cords note, *Leopard's Spots* "fed [to] northern audiences [Dixon's] mythical version of Reconstruction history from a New York stage in 1903." Gerster and Cords add that "not only did Broadway accept [Dixon's] version of the southern past, but the production was the hit of the theatrical season" (55).

Chesnutt's resistance to Dixon's racist ideology began in relation to *Leopard's* and, I would argue, culminated with *Birth*. In relation to *Leopard's*, Chesnutt became acutely aware of the political importance of *The Marrow of Tradition* (1901), his own historical novel about the Wilmington riot, could play in presenting the riot from an African American perspective. Having entertained high hopes for *Marrow's* being recognized as an impartial rendering of the effects of racism in the aftermath of a harrowing historical event, Chesnutt was forced to take note of the largely negative reception of the novel;[2] subsequently, he sought ways to bring his novel to the attention of high-ranking political figures: five potentially sympathetic members of the House of Representatives to whom he sent copies of his novel in 1902. Though the representatives' views of *Marrow* varied, in general, the three responses he received agreed that both Dixon's and Chesnutt's fictionalized versions of the riot held credibility and served to balance one another. Chesnutt was not satisfied with their responses, and his vehemence against racists, especially Southern racists—of which he considered Dixon a preeminent example—persisted.[3] As pointed out by Eric Sundquist, Chesnutt "regularly took more openly radical stands than many other black leaders [concerning the injustice of Southern whites against blacks]" (422). In a stinging comment to Washington about the disenfranchisement of Southern blacks, Chesnutt writes of those with whom he shares his heritage: "I wish them well [Southern whites], and first of all I wish that they may learn to do justice. . . . I admire your Christ-like spirit in loving the Southern whites, but I confess I am not up to it" (qtd. in Sundquist 422).[4] It is, then, Chesnutt's well-formed conscience, the same sense of justice that compelled him to write *Marrow* to set straight the historical backdrop of the Wilmington Riot of 1898, that will urge him to produce a work that forefronts the dishonor of the Southern aristocracy in relation to the legacy of slavery. Though *Paul Marchand* proves not to be a deliberate revisioning of *Birth*, it is a subtle satire on the Southern traditions that underpinned race slavery and that were invoked to justify the social and political aftermath of the institution.

The fact that *Paul Marchand* was rejected by Houghton, Harcourt, and Knopf within a two-month period must have been less related to its being out-of-vogue local color writing, as Dean McWilliams has argued,[5] than to the political climate of the 1921 post–World War I United States, which was conducive to reinforcing stereotypes of non- and unassimilated whites.[6] *Birth,* after all, is itself blatant plantation fiction with an absurd twist—obviously white actors pose in blackface as black characters; yet, as Ronald J. Green stresses, *Birth* is "the first American blockbuster" (xiii), and its racist hyperbole was taken seriously, as all accounts of the aftermath of its screenings attest. Chesnutt made the connection between the national mood and *Birth*'s depiction of black soldiers the focus of his protest letter to Ohio's governor concerning the film. Chesnutt was especially critical of *Birth*'s portrayal of black Union soldiers' spurious conduct; particularly unsettling to Chesnutt was the characterization of the film's antagonist, Gus, a mulatto captain of a black regiment, the would-be rapist of a white girl. In relation to his concern about the film's depiction of black soldiers, Chesnutt wrote a letter of protest against the showing of *Birth* in Cleveland, Chesnutt's hometown, calling to mind the patriotism of black troops in World War I before making a strong case against the "vicious and anti-social character" of a film that is "devoted to exploiting the alleged misconduct of colored Union soldiers during the reconstruction period" (*Exemplary* 133–134).[7] This further reinforces my point that *Paul Marchand* is a demonstration against the negative message about blacks, especially males (and, coincidentally, the positive one relating to white males and females), in *The Birth of a Nation* and that it is, especially, intended to raise questions about assumptions of character based solely on race. *The Birth of a Nation*, a production that was effectively the birth of the film industry, likely served as Chesnutt's muse for finishing and submitting *Paul Marchand* for publication after a sixteen-year hiatus from writing novels.[8]

PAUL MARCHAND, F.M.C.: A CLOSE-UP

The historical backdrop of *Paul Marchand* is only part of my reason for arguing that Chesnutt intended the novel as a response to *Birth*.[9] I recognize Chesnutt's intention for *Paul Marchand, F.M.C.* not as an undeviating trope of *Birth*, but rather as a decidedly subtler response to the patent exaggeration of the latter. *Paul Marchand* contains a dark mystery concerning the identity of the legal heir to wealthy plantation owner Pierre Beaurepas's estate, the key to which is held by an inscrutable, secretive San Dominican freed-slave woman, Zabet Philosophe. It offers action-filled scenes charged with danger and suspense, scenes that could easily compete with some of the sensational footage in *Birth*. The novel portrays a love story—Paul's marriage to his mulatta wife, Julie, which is legally nullified when it is determined that he is white. It also includes a romance—Philippe Beaurepas's relationship with Josephine Morales, which does not revolve around melodrama but, rather, honor (into this romance is integrated the rescue of Josephine, not by Philippe but by Paul). In addition, a quadroon ball "of unparalleled splendor" is included as the centerpiece of the novel (64).

But *Paul Marchand* is decidedly more than a suspense story with a happy ending. Threading its way through the novel is the theme of honor, a theme that pervades many of Chesnutt's works, questioning the meaning of honor by deriding the master class for whom the term "honor" is deemed a birthright. In contrast to *Birth,* however, *Paul Marchand* bases all questions of honor not on color, codes, or traditions, but on character, and reinforces the role that race slavery engendered in corrupting the meaning of honor. And while *Paul Marchand* readily competes on various levels with *Birth*, the novel's message takes precedence over any other characteristic in the work. It is more extravagant than Chesnutt's conjure tales and short stories (though obviously less provocative than his novel *The Marrow of Tradition,* which failed in the white marketplace); yet, arguably, it is one of his more candid novels in terms of the ramifications of racism, especially in relation to family ties, stemming from slavery. *Paul Marchand* has a complicated plot imbued with subtle irony and satire, hallmarks of Chesnutt's talent for couching political arguments in his fiction. The reader must remain mindful of Chesnutt's acute perception when recognizing the novel's significance and its potential as a controlled but profound race novel, one that tropes the blackface minstrelsy in *Birth* by creating an honorable, credible "black" character who is biologically white (and who, it might be important to note, would appear visibly so on stage or screen). While *Paul Marchand* does not deal directly with one of the most harmful themes of Dixon's *The Leopard's Spots* (1902) and *The Clansman* (1905), and, most disturbingly, in *Birth*—the atavism of black males and the consequent danger to the chastity of innocent white females—it does include a dramatic episode involving a revenge plot, Josephine Morales, Paul Marchand, and two black male characters.

Instead of depicting the Reconstruction era as a venue for urging the restoration of an antebellum (both the Civil War and World War I) racial order (and, by extension, an ethnic hierarchy) as, arguably, does *Birth, Paul Marchand* resolutely takes the reader back to the antebellum South to assess the underpinnings of the race issues that persisted in the twentieth century. One issue close to the light-complexioned Chesnutt's own sense of racial injustice is preeminent in *Paul Marchand*: the practice of color coding people rather than judging them by their characters. *Birth* reinforces this notion, portraying virtually all black characters in a negative light by focusing on the lustful natures of two black characters: Gus, the black Union soldier, would-be rapist of Flora, the innocent younger sister of the film's hero, the "Little Colonel," Confederate Colonel Ben Cameron (Flora jumps over a cliff to her death to escape her pursuer); and Silas Lynch, a mulatto carpetbagger, who lusts after the film's heroine, Elsie Stoneman, and abducts her. (She is saved by Ben Cameron.) Chesnutt undercuts the very notion of reducing the concept of honor to the color of one's skin in *Paul Marchand* by proving that color is an indefinite signifier, especially in relation to the institution of slavery in the antebellum South. Race slavery seemingly made it possible to separate potential slaves—blacks—from those exempt from enslavement—whites. History, however, informs us that as the complexions of slaves became increasingly lighter—the result of miscegenation—methods of identifying blacks, other than visual perception, were necessary to preserve white primogeniture and all of the privileges, including social, economic, and legal, that accompanied whiteness. Whiteness, then, was the only viable gauge of true honor, the other side of *Birth's* representation of blacks. For this reason, Paul Marchand, the eponymous hero of Chesnutt's novel, serves as the perfect medium through which the audience is forced to re-view the meaning of honor and, consequently, its antithesis: Paul is white but is reared as a quadroon in 1820s New Orleans. Although he is a "free man of color," his life consists of daily imputations against his manhood and his humanity, making Paul metaphorically a white slave.

By the end of the novel, Paul achieves selfhood. In addition, he proves what honor is and is not, as well as who is and is not honorable, after a series of incidents. Through the novel's dialogue, narrative, and performance, the reader and Paul are led to the truth, if not a solution, for the race-based complications introduced in the novel, truths that belie the portrayals in *Birth*. Through Paul Marchand, we can deconstruct the discourse of the majority, refocus on their motives and actions, and arrive, along with Paul, at a place that allows for the rethinking of the meaning of honor, which, after all, is the point on which we Americans, in large part, base our most hallowed personal, societal, and legislative decisions. And Chesnutt's novel accomplishes this constructive look at racial issues without, it could be argued, making a ripple on the surface of society, unlike *Birth*, which caused waves of antagonism.

As Vincent F. Rocchio points out, the opening scene of *Birth* "introduces race as central to the narrative," focusing on the differences between black slaves and their white masters in terms of positioning: slaves are "stand[ing] passively," "gazing intently," or "glancing furtively" at their white, well-dressed masters who exude confidence and power in contrast to the uncertain attitude of the slaves (32–33). *Paul Marchand* opens, instead, with a montage of New Orleans' picturesque *vieux carre* and offers a brief historical background of the city that includes an introduction of the antebellum New Orleans hierarchy, the cynosure of the novel's complication. The audience is invited to view the colorful scene as the narrator pans Jackson Square, describing the bustle of the street and the city's diverse population, beginning with the top of the social/racial hierarchy:

the French Creoles, who look down on the Spanish Creoles, are the scions. They
have

their own very proud and exclusive society. . . . They were the professional men and
the owners of land and slaves, the rentiers, or gentlemen of independent income.
Descending by easy grades, there were the people of color—octoroons, quadroons,
mulattoes—many of them small tradesmen, a few of them large merchants or planters,
and more than one the inheritor of substantial means from a white father or grandfather—an inferior but not entirely degraded class. . . . At the basis of all lay the black
slaves whose arduous and unrequited toil, upon the broad, deep-soiled plantations of
indigo, rice, cotton, and sugar cane furnished the wherewithal to maintain the wealth
and luxury of capital. (6–7)

In contrast to *Birth*'s insistence upon duality, *Paul Marchand* troubles the perceptions of black and white which continued to reverberate in twentieth-century
America.

The first chapter also introduces the intriguing Zabet Philosophe, who freely
engages in dialogue with the city's professional men as they go about their business. Importantly, Chesnutt narrates this section of the work through Zabet's
shrewd observations. On the square where Zabet sells pralines, she speaks with
the Beaurepas cousins, nephews to her employer, Pierre Beaurepas, as well as to
Paul Marchand, her master's unacknowledged legitimate son, providing the reader with information regarding the elderly Beaurepas's plan to ensure that his estate
is passed down to his legitimate heir, Paul. For complicated reasons hinging on
his mother and father's false sense of honor, Paul was remanded to the custody
of an octoroon woman who reared him as her own son.[10] Zabet's conversations
with the Beurepas cousins are particularly significant in disclosing the ignoble nature of four of the five white Creole cousins, brothers Raoul, Henri, and Hector
Beaurepas, and a second pair of brothers, Adolphe and Philippe Beaurepas.
Zabet encourages each cousin's belief that he will soon inherit his Uncle Pierre
Beaurepas's estate and wealth, and all but Philippe wish for their uncle's swift
departure, for all are mired in debt due to mismanagement of the money already
provided by their uncle. Only Philippe's assets remain liquid, and Philippe's desire to become the Beaurepas heir is based on the heir's right to marry Josephine
Morales, the woman Philippe loves. Josephine's father, Jose Morales, it should be
noted, is heavily indebted to Pierre Beaurepas, his plantation mortgaged to him;
however, the Morales/Beaurepas tie was originally one based on an act of honor:
Morales saved Pierre's life.

Chesnutt seems intent in *Paul Marchand* to expose not only the Old South's
ill-used race-based taxonomy of character, but also a few of the questionable

practices among "gentlemen" of the era, rituals that excluded black men altogether, though not necessarily to their disadvantage. The scene occurs on the *vieux carre* in the opening of the novel, although it is placed in the second chapter, a chapter that introduces Paul Marchand. It is a scene that requires the audience's full attention, and one that merges the ideology of the antebellum setting of the novel with continuing Jim Crow practices of the early twentieth century as it emphasizes the novel's focus on race and honor. It is a scene that anticipates Paul's emerging sense of self as a man who refuses to be bound by a code of color and illustrates his apprehension of whites' misconception of honor. The scene transpires prior to the audience's knowledge of Paul, which is significant. As Paul Marchand and Raoul Beaurepas, only mere acquaintances at this point in the novel, happen to be walking toward each other on the street, they "come into personal contact" with one another (15). Marchand, not named but described through the eyes of Zabet, who continues to serve as an important medium in the unfolding of Marchand's story, is "a handsome young man of middle height, with a proud expression, tinged with a melancholy discontent." (15). Immediately upon contact, both men, who have been distracted, apparently by Josephine Morales and her father as they approach the nearby church, regain focus, and Paul "draws back deprecatingly murmuring an apology" (15). With a truculent air, Raoul "involuntarily" slaps Paul across the face, calls him a scoundrel in French, and tells him that he should "keep to the gutter" if he cannot avoid the path of a gentleman. He adds that if Paul would keep his eyes in front of him instead of on white ladies he would fare better, and he adds that he is sure Paul will require further lessons "to learn his place" (15).

The perceptive reader might deduce much from the description of Paul's body language and might identify him as "black." For other astute observers, the adverbs and adjectives describing the men's actions would be telling—the deprecating murmur of apology, the truculent air, the involuntary slap, and the accusation against Paul's position as gentleman. But mention of walking in gutters and averting one's eyes from white women would be the clincher for most Southern audiences. Those failing to historicize the scene could overlook all of these signs and might think Paul Marchand a coward for not retaliating after his face is slapped. But the scene is far more complicated than it appears to be, and further discussion of several aspects of this performance as it relates to Paul's developing sense of self is crucial.

In historical context, the slap, if between two white "gentlemen," would effect a duel, made imperative by the Code of Honor of the Old South. Although this does not transpire, witnesses to the incident expect that it will: "the bystanders [*who*] *did not know the two men*, held their breaths for a moment, in anticipation of the tragedy which would in all probability follow so grievous an insult. . . . Among the Creole French and Spanish the point of honor was jealously guarded and frequent resort was had to the code for its maintenance" (16, emphasis added). Following the bystanders' cue, the reader continues to puzzle over the performance of these two apparently white gentlemen. The Code Duelo, the convention demanding that gentlemen settle a "grievous insult" (16), such as being slapped, is overridden in this instance by the Code Noir, which forbids a black man to strike a white man on pain of losing liberty or even life (17). In addition, the Black Codes forbade blacks to carry arms. And the term "gentleman" would not be used in describing a black man during this antebellum setting under any circumstances, but in Raoul's self-description, the term "gentleman" would imply that he is superior to Paul Marchand in any number of ways. The term destabilizes when we learn that all of the Gentlemen Beaurepas are dissipated to one extent or another—they gamble, are frivolous with money, losing it in a variety of ways including injudicious speculations, Raoul's forte, and sell their children by slave mistresses. As pointed out above, Philippe alone is debt free. We recognize just how powerful class and race were, however, in establishing the antebellum South's code of ethics when we read antebellum intellectual William J. Grayson's observation that "swearing, gambling, drinking, wenching, and lying along with accumulating debts without intending to pay them . . . are not incompatible with the character of a man of honor" (qtd. in Wyatt-Brown 23). Paul Marchand is not misguided by the established white supremacist codes, however, which leads to my second point about this performance.

The slap scene in *Paul Marchand* is further illuminated by Samira Kawash's discussion on Douglas Sirk's 1959 film version of Fanny Hurst's novel, *Imitation of Life*. Kawash focuses on the scene in which Sarah Jane, the young black female in the film who is passing for white, is slapped and forced to the ground by her white boyfriend, Frankie, upon his discovery of Sarah Jane's racial background. His slap, argues Kawash, becomes more relevant to the preservation of the color line, as depicted variously in the film, when related to Walter Benjamin's 1921 work, "Critique of Violence." In terms of "Critique," the slap is "law-preserving violence": the law surrounding the color line, one of tradition if not formal code, is reinforced and conserved by Frankie's violence. It is the "racializing violence that insists on Sarah Jane's blackness and the supremacist violence that enforces the separation and superiority of whiteness" (Kawash 17). But the slap also serves to found the law of separation of races in what Benjamin would call "lawmaking violence," which is "outside the realm of law" (Kawash 17). Kawash follows the "performativity of the law's distinction that the color line names"; Frankie's slap blurs the boundary between founding and enforcing violence, "reveal[ing] Sarah Jane's 'true blackness' *and* mak[ing] Sarah Jane 'black'" (17, emphasis added). Her argument follows Jacques Derrida's in showing that "conservation in its turn refounds, so that it can conserve what it claims to found" (qtd. in Kawash 17).

Similar to Frankie's act of violence against Sarah Jane, Raoul's slapping Paul Marchand, especially in public in the novel's context, conserves a law while it attempts to reestablish the law of complete separation of races, one that Chesnutt showcases as an absurdity, for what it reestablishes and conserves is a lie: Paul is, in *fact* and *appearance*, white, but is thought to be black by those who know who he is (including Raoul); he is thus "mistaken" for white by the bystanders who do not know who he is and expect to see him respond to the insult as any white gentleman would. Even though Paul's case is a special one—he is white and, ironically, is "passing" for black—the point is well made: the laws of the time were enforcing and refounding the "lie" of race through the one-drop rule, whereby one part African heritage "dishonored" thirty-one parts Caucasian heritage, affecting everything from marriage contracts (a law that will affect Paul and his family profoundly), to property ownership, to the denial of blacks serving as jurors. The performance lasts only briefly, but it speaks volumes.

Two other scenes in the novel contend with *Birth* in terms of grandeur and spectacle; moreover, they advance Chesnutt's theme of the meaning of honor. The first of these, set forth in the chapter titled "The Quadroon Ball," adds a touch of opulence, in contrast to the spectacle pervading *Birth,* but also represents a class of African Americans that would challenge the notion of black atavism, especially in relation to miscegenation, that *Birth* forefronts as a reason for regaining white supremacy. In doing so, the scene supplies further indication of the dishonorable behavior of the New Orleans scions. It especially discloses the hypocrisy of miscegenation, the result of which was the fracturing of families, the dispossession of children, and an increasingly "white" free black and slave population, while it emphasizes the fact that white men were exempt from honoring their own marriage vows while they determined the laws concerning intermarriage. With historical accuracy, the ball is described in some detail. The setting of the ball, housed in a building on Conde Street, is resplendent:

The large ballroom, profusely decorated with cut flowers and potted palms, was lighted by a grand chandelier with dozens of wax candles and crystal pendants shivering with the vibration of the dance, and flashing with all the colors of the spectrum.... [M]ost of the women were young and shapely, many of them not casually distinguishable from white, and the men, also for the most part young, were of the cream of New Orleans society. (71–72)

The ball, a masked affair, is attended by white male aristocrats: the narrator explains that "no amount of wealth or education could qualify a male quadroon for this gathering of the cream of his own womanhood" (66). Further historical commentary is provided to enlighten the audience on particular circumstances underpinning the yearly fete. The beautiful quadroon women are the product of slaves and their French and Spanish Creole slave masters who observed the "fashion . . . to manumit the children of these . . . unions, and to provide for their support. There had thus grown up in New Orleans the large class of free colored people known as the quadroon caste" (64–65). Paul Marchand and his wife, Julie Lenoir Marchand, are both members of this class.

The quadroon women, who "vied with the white Creole women in beauty, in dress, and in graceful dancing," were the reason for the ball. Attired in glamorous gowns, they attended the ball for the purpose of establishing sexual liaisons— "they were meat for [the] masters"—which afforded these women of color some opportunity for security and wealth for which they could not otherwise hope (66):

They gained freedom, ease, sometimes a love, which, whatever it may have lacked of the romantic devotion which goes by that name, preserved them from the pains of poverty and brought to their children beauty and brains and sometimes wealth. (65–66)

Drama pervades the scene after Paul Marchand is dispatched by his wife, Julie, to retrieve her younger sister, Lizette, from the quadroon ball to which Lizette has gone without permission. Paul's sister-in-law, though "carefully brought up," exhibits a "touch of waywardness. . . . Vain, frivolous, beautiful in the quadroon way, the blood of the gay Creole gentlemen and their dusky sweethearts throbbed in her veins in a ceaseless demand for excitement, gaiety, pleasure" (68). At risk to his own life—black men were prohibited from the quadroon balls "under pain of death"—Marchand gains entrance to the ball disguised in a half-mask. Paul reaches Lizette just prior to the unmasking event that will disclose the young woman's identity and, as a result, dishonor herself and her family. However, a visiting French Duke, with whom Paul had briefly come in contact while studying in Paris, and Henri Beaurepas are both smitten with Lizette, and Beaurepas, recognizing Paul, intervenes before Paul and Lizette can exit the ball. Paul is thrown outside, pistol whipped, and jailed for his crime. Fortunately, Philippe Beaurepas intercedes before Hector Beaurepas forces Lizette to unmask, and the young woman returns home with her reputation intact.

Chesnutt's focus on the quadroon ball is important in relaying historical information to the audience. It rewinds the story of miscegenation, concentrating the lens on the practices of those whose power created a biracial population, white males—especially the aristocratic class—and it undermines the mostly negative portrayal of biracial men and women in the literature and art of the era's popular culture: specifically in *Birth*. It does not, however, simply signify on those portrayals. Chesnutt does not seem interested, for example, in responding to *Birth*'s depiction of Congressman Stoneman's mulatto housekeeper, Lydia Brown, whom Rocchio describes as "throwing a hysterical, orgiastic fit" that "strongly suggests a kind of animalistic sexuality" after her aspirations to ascend the social ladder are dashed by a white senator's snub (39). The quadroon ball is nothing if not decorous, at least on the surface, as the institution of slavery itself was popularly portrayed. Paul Marchand's removal from the ball is deftly achieved without the guests' notice. And, while Lizette may not be a ready adherent to Marchand's strict code of honor, she takes it seriously enough to "implore" Hector Beaurepas to refrain from removing her mask in front of the Duke and to allow her to leave the ball after Paul is evicted from the premises. Lizette, unlike *Birth*'s Lydia Brown, is characterized as being significantly more civilized than the predatory white aristocrats surrounding her at the quadroon ball.

The most spectacular scene in the novel includes murder, arson, the threat of flood, and the rescue of Josephine Morales. Responsible for the mayhem are two free black men, unable to prove their status, who are falsely jailed for vagrancy. This occurs after Mendoza, Don Jose Morales's cruel overseer, brutally beats and captures them for trespassing on *Trois Pigeons*, the Morales plantation. The two escape jail and perpetrate their revenge plot against *Trois Pigeons*. Although the scene compares loosely to sensational scenes in *Birth*, it differs in important ways.[11] *Birth* is, at core, a racist film, and its spectacular scenes are used to stress essential racial differences between black and white characters, almost exclusively condemning blacks and recommending whites: blacks, unless closely associated with their former white masters, are savages; whites are civilized; blacks are lascivious; whites are chaste; blacks are impulsive; whites are restrained. All of these characteristics relay the message that whites must control blacks.

Chesnutt, more fairly (and, the student of history would argue, more accurately), does not avoid assigning negative characteristics to black characters, but he equally delineates white characters with like qualities. For example, Paul knows the treachery the two blacks are willing to effect on *Trois Pigeons* and its inhabitants: these two men "would live only to gratify strong passions—lust and drink and gaming and revenge" (156). These are the same passions ascribed to white characters, mostly aristocrats, throughout *Paul Marchand*; and, at this point in the plot, the passionate nature of white characters has been effectively exemplified, particularly among the Beaurepas males.

As Paul gallops onto the set of the destruction of *Trois Pigeons*, he is surrounded by the sights and sounds of chaos. In front of him are the men running toward the damaged levee with shovels in hand to repair the break and contain the flood waters; peripherally, he catches the shadow of a figure running toward the house, which, momentarily, he sees in flames; and toward him Mendoza gallops up asking for Paul's assistance, and from him learns that Morales and his slaves are those working to repair the levee. As the two men ride toward the house they hear shrieking and see a "huge mulatto dash from the house with a woman's limp form thrown across his shoulder" (158); Mendoza runs into the house to douse the fire, only to meet the remaining marauder who "brains him with an ax" (158). Despite the edge-of-the-seat action, suspense, and violence at this point, authorial intrusion interrupts the narrative's progress to deliver a moral concerning Mendoza's violent death:[12]

The overseer had lived by violence. He had made himself the instrument of the greed and avarice of others; he had done the dirty work of slavery and had paid the price at the hands of one of the victims of the system [the black desperado]. We never borrow but we must pay. Sooner or later the scales are balanced. (158)

Here as elsewhere in the novel, Chesnutt reminds his audience that victims and victimizers are as indistinguishable from one another in a slaveocracy as is differentiating white from black or attributing negative or positive qualities exclusively to either race. *Paul Marchand* the novel and Paul Marchand the man are poised to disrupt all race-based assumptions

As in *Birth*, preserving the chastity of an innocent woman takes precedence over all other considerations. The narrator makes clear that the destruction of *Trois Pigeons* affects Paul intimately: the plantation is, at this point in the novel, his property, for he has already been advised that he is the legitimate white heir of Pierre Beaurepas; nonetheless, the "danger to Josephine dwarfed every other thought" (156). To this end, Paul risks his life to rescue Josephine and nearly loses his own in the process, almost being dispatched by Mendoza's assassin. Instead, Paul impales the murderer on his sword just before the mulatto who holds Josephine escapes from the scene. Importantly, the mulatto who has the opportunity to slash Josephine's throat before he escapes, "with a lingering remnant of pity [throws] her body to the ground and disappear[s] into the underbrush . . . to be as long as he lived the bane of the society which had produced him" (160). Chesnutt is tenacious in balancing the scales of justice in *Paul Marchand*.

This balancing of justice in the novel is complex: it is never readily reduced to black and white, and, in part, it revolves around pay back—both in terms of revenge *and* of compensation. The event of Paul rescuing Josephine from the renegade mulatto absolves Pierre Beaurepas's debt to Morales for having saved his life. But Paul's moral act results also in the juxtaposition of his character and Morales's, to the further detriment of Morales's. In addition to Morales's gross mismanagement of money, Morales treats his daughter, Josephine, as chattel: the narrator relates that "her fate had been fixed almost from her birth. She was the price of *Trois Pigeons* and no man not able to lift its mortgage might dare raise his eyes to her. . . . Josephine was frankly in the market, for sale to the highest bidder" (170). And Paul Marchand has automatically paid that price: he is the son and rightful heir of Pierre Beaurepas. Morales directs Paul, "Take [Josephine], my boy. It was your father's wish [to rectify the debt owed him] and my promise; and more, she is yours by right of conquest"—Paul's saving *Trois Pigeons* and Josephine's chastity and life (161). This bartering of Josephine, incidentally, overrides Josephine's desire to marry the man she loves, Philippe Beaurepas. At this point, the romance, the love story, and the theme of honor intersect, bringing the novel to its conclusion.

Despite the temptation of being allowed to marry a beautiful white Creole woman, Paul ultimately remains with his quadroon wife, Julie, although his marriage to her is legally nullified upon disclosure of his pure white heritage. His rationale for keeping intact his marriage is part and parcel of his experiences living as a quadroon as well as the discourse surrounding him. Paul's sense of self emerges as a direct result of his environment: he has heard the word "honor" bandied about by the white Creole society around him, and specifically by the Beaurepas men before he becomes their acknowledged cousin; and he has seen the actions related to the term "honor," both in the United States South and in Paris, where he was educated. Paul Marchand, a man of true honor in his decision to preserve his marriage contract, foregoes the Beaurepas legacy. He argues that he is likely one of a kind in Louisiana—"the legitimate son of a good family . . . condemned by his parents to an inferior class solely to gratify a woman's selfish pride and a man's sentimental weakness—if not callous indifference—and then after many years recalled to his own race and family" (175–176). Marchand has been adequately influenced by what he has witnessed, experienced, and discussed himself during his life; his decision to stay with his wife is based on pride—but it is selfless—and sentimentality, but certainly not on weakness.

Marchand relinquishes his role as controller of the Beaurepas estate to Philippe, who it may be assumed is Zabet's grandson, son of Pierre Beaurepas's brother Renee and Zabet's daughter, both owned by Renee. As a result, Paul achieves revenge on two levels: first, he leaves the estate to a black male, thus undermining the one-drop rule, the upshot of which is that although he does reveal that one cousin has African ancestry, he does not divulge which; and second, he successfully fulfills the Beaurepas's own *coup pour coup*, blow for blow, Code of Honor. Paul retaliates to each Beaurepas cousins' offense against him when he was recognized as a quadroon—Raoul's slapping him, Hector's cheating him out of his bid for cotton and adding insult to injury by calling him a "pig of a negro" and threatening to slit his ears, and Henri throwing Paul out of the quadroon ball, having him knocked unconscious, and jailing him. Each cousin meets Paul in a duel during which Paul effects the letter of the Beaurepas's motto: he slashes

Raoul's cheek, slits Hector's ear, and nearly hamstrings Henri; however, the reader recognizes that Paul is more civilized than all of those who have insisted that he define himself as one deserving to live only on the fringes of society. After each of the egregious acts against him, Paul is left in impotent rage, the mitigation of which lies in his being able to relate it to his wife. After his incarceration, for example, when Julie mentions the merits of her own white father whose legacy she and Paul and their children are enjoying, he responds in the same manner as whites have historically responded to the possibility of individual blacks serving as gauges of their own race: "They are merely the exceptions that prove the rule. . . . They despise us, and I hate them all, each according to his own degree of scorn" (91). He tells her at this point that he will have revenge.

As it turns out, Paul Marchand overcomes his unreserved malice because choice is factored into the situation through his father's legacy to him—wealth and his newly minted white self. At this point, though he takes two weeks to consider all his options and their alternatives, Paul Marchand makes the honorable choice—to remain "black" and, thus, to remain legally married to Julie; consequently, he retains his pride and publicly demonstrates his love for his children. His choice is not, however, without reservation; he chooses to abandon the inferior position of the quadroon in Louisiana and moves his family to Paris, where he has the opportunity to be treated equally, a fitting comment on the state of race relations in twentieth-century America from the perspective of a white aristocrat who has endured the hardships of a dispossessed race.

When Chesnutt attempted to publish *Paul Marchand, F.M.C.,* he believed the time was ripe for his fictionalized attempt to reconcile the myth and reality surrounding race relations in early twentieth-century America, particularly in light of the burgeoning popularity and powerful persuasiveness of film, specifically of *The Birth of a Nation.* But, while Chesnutt continued politically to influence positively the place of African Americans in society, his fiction remained ahead of its time; and white mainstream American society was not prepared to accept any work that questioned, even remotely, white supremacy in the post–World War I environment. Consequently, *Paul Marchand* was to remain unpublished until the end of the twentieth century, and we are only now able to consider what role Chesnutt's novel may have played in its historical context.

NOTES

1. See *The Journals of Charles W. Chesnutt,* ed. Richard H. Brodhead: Using literature as a vehicle, Chesnutt promised to be "one of the first to head a determined, organized crusade" against such a "barrier to the moral progress of the American people" as their "spirit of caste which is so insidious as to pervade a whole nation" (139).

2. See *"To Be an Author": Letters of Charles W. Chesnutt, 1889–190,* ed. Joseph R. McElrath Jr. and Robert C. Leitz III. (172 n.1). During its first year of publication, *Leopard's* sold 105,000 copies. By contrast, Chesnutt's *The Marrow of Tradition* (1901), also a historical fictionalization of the Wilmington riot, sold only 3,000 copies after its first year. See also T. Thomas Fortune's praise of *Marrow* in *"To Be an Author";* Fortune calls the novel "the strongest work of fiction on our side since *Uncle Tom's Cabin"* (169).

3. See Chesnutt's *"To Be an Author,"* 185–189, for the complete letter to Washington from which this comment was abstracted.

4. Chesnutt, in a letter to E. J. Lilly, dated October 16, 1916, writing about the poor reception of *Colonel's* (1905), provides a disarmingly incisive comment about his historical fiction: "Unfortunately for my writings, they were on the unpopular side of the race question, and any success they may have had must have been due to their merit" (Chesnutt, *Exemplary Citizen,* 126). In apparent response to Lilly's assertion that Chesnutt was a superior writer to Dixon, Chesnutt remonstrates less obliquely that Dixon, "who took the other side, was not satisfied to present it [the race question] fairly, but made a fortune prostituting his talent to ignoble uses" (126).

5. For Dean McWilliams's observations on the rejection of *Paul Marchand,* see his introduction to the book (x and xv).

6. See Susan Gilman, "Micheaux's Chesnutt," especially 1084, for an insightful argument that relates black filmmaker Oscar Micheaux's *Within Our Gates* (1919–20) and Chesnutt's *Marrow* to the political climate in the post–World War I era.

7. This letter was sent to William R. Green, a fellow member of the Rowfant Club and a long-term member of the Cleveland Chamber of Commerce, of which Chesnutt was also a member. The letter addresses the United States' entry into World War I in relation to the loyalty of black soldiers and, as related in the text, specifically denounces *Birth's* depiction of the "principal villain of the story, the would-be rapist . . . portrayed as a colored captain in the Union army" not only because of its flagrant and inflammatory racism, but because "with war declared there will undoubtedly be a large accession [to the honorable black regiments in the regular army]." Chesnutt adds that the film's depiction is "an insult to the national uniform when worn by men of color, as the public exhibition of such a picture as *The Birth of a Nation,* which, as a work of pictorial art is a superb and impressive thing, and all the more vicious for that reason, should not be permitted at this time, when all citizens should stand together to support the honor of the nation" (*Exemplary Citizen,* 134).

8. It was also a pivotal point for black activism, including that of black writers. The racial violence that resulted after the screening of *Birth* in virtually every city of its performance created an ongoing campaign among the black intelligentsia, most notably by members of the NAACP, to censor the movie after its initial Los Angeles screening in 1915 and a concomitant drive to counter the film's wholly negative characterization of postbellum blacks with more positive, accurate characterizations via black theatrical performances and film. For more on this subject see David Levering Lewis, especially 509, concerning W.E B. Du Bois and Angelina Grimke's efforts; and J. Ronald Green, 106 and 146–147, concerning Booker T. Washington's effort. Chesnutt was himself actively engaged in the political crusade against *Birth.* In 1915, Chesnutt prompted Ohio's governor to "exercise [his] authority" to ensure that a large group of Ohio youths be deterred from viewing a Philadelphia showing of *Birth* while touring Pennsylvania on a state-sponsored trip. The governor publicly agreed with Chesnutt (*Exemplary Citizen,* 122). See also on this subject Ernestine Williams Pickens, *Charles W. Chesnutt and the Progressive Movement Chesnutt* (New York: Pace UP, 1994).

9. Chesnutt may have had some hope that its publication and successful sales would serve as a precursor to its adaptation into a stage play and/or screenplay that would become a classic that would reach a wide audience—more of the appeal of Stowe's *Uncle Tom's Cabin* than Dixon's *Clansman* or Griffith's *Birth.* My reason for suggesting this rests, in part, on Chesnutt's ongoing

relationship with Oscar Micheaux, who adapted *House behind the Cedars* into a film version in 1925, followed in 1932 by a sound version, titled *The Veiled Aristocrats*, as well as his continued general interest in writing screenplays and stage scenarios.

10. Although the scenario surrounding the dispossession of Paul is complicated, it serves well to illustrate the lengths to which the aristocracy would go to ensure its "good name," regardless of the means taken to secure it. It involves Paul's parents marrying and conceiving Paul before his mother actually becomes the widow of her first husband. The plan to "adopt" Paul, who had been placed in the care of a quadroon nurse by Paul's parents until they could reveal their marriage publicly (thus retaining their reputation by apparently following convention) was foiled when Paul's five orphaned Beaurepas cousins are remanded to Pierre's care. Thus, they become legal "blood" relatives of Beaurepas. Making an adopted son heir to an estate instead of a living blood relative would fly in the face of the code of honor, expressly of primogeniture; hence, Paul, although provided an education and a stipend, as were some dispossessed children of white fathers and slave mothers, remained the unacknowledged "quadroon" son of unknown origin until the disclosure of his patrimony.

11. Scenes that epitomize the spectacle pervading *Birth* include (1) the raid on Piedmont scene, in which the Confederate army rides in to quell the behavior of a marauding group of black soldiers, led by a white captain; (2) the chase scene that ends in the lynching of Gus, the mulatto who pursues Flora Cameron, ostensibly to rape her; (3) the abduction of Elsie Stoneman by Silas Green, followed by her rescue by Ben Cameron; and (4) the final scene, a return to order that includes a grand parade of the Ku Klux Klan on horseback with their faithful women walking by their sides in a show of white supremacy.

12. The fact that *Paul Marchand* includes several such intrusions, including the explanation of Paul's parents' deception concerning him, does not preclude its being suitable for a screenplay. All such intrusions in the novel are important messages relating to racism and/or the theme of honor, and such authorial intrusions in films of the time were a common practice. Silent films and talkies provided background and historical information via intertitles, a form of authorial interjection. More direct authorial intrusion was practiced by Micheaux and others. See Bowser and Spence, *Writing Himself into History*, especially 142. The authors explain that "authorial intrusion such as the list of heroic battles mentioned in *Within Our Gates*, or, in other films, a character's declamation against gambling, sloth, or immorality, moments when the author seems to be preaching, lecturing, or educating, disrupt the fictional flow of the drama.... Yet despite this intrusion ... Micheaux's fictional universe is ultimately ordered by a tidy resolution" (142).

WORKS CITED

Bowser, Pearl, and Louise Spence, *Writing Himself into History: Oscar Micheaux, His Silent Films, and His Audiences*. New Brunswick, NJ: Rutgers UP, 2000.

Chesnutt, Charles. *An Exemplary Citizen: Letters of Charles W. Chesnutt, 1906–1932*. Ed. Jesse S. Crisler, Robert C. Leitz III, and Joseph R. McElrath Jr. Stanford, CA: Stanford UP, 2002.

———. *The Journals of Charles W. Chesnutt*. Ed. Richard H. Brodhead. Durham, Duke UP, 1993.

———. *Paul Marchand, F.M.C.* Ed. Dean McWilliams. Princeton: Princeton UP, 1999.

———. *"To Be an Author": Letters of Charles W. Chesnutt, 1889–190*. Ed. Joseph R. McElrath Jr. and Robert C. Leitz III. Princeton: Princeton UP, 1997.

Chesnutt, Helen M. *Charles Waddell Chesnutt: Pioneer of the Color Line*. Chapel Hill: U of North Carolina P, 1952.

Gerster, Patrick, and Nicholas Cords. "The Northern Origins of Southern Mythology." *Myth and Southern History: The New South*. 2nd ed. Ed. Patrick Gerster and Nicholas Cords. Urbana and Chicago: U of Illinois P, 1989.

Gilman, Susan. "Micheaux's Chesnutt." *PMLA* 114.5 (1999): 1080–1088.

Green, Ronald J. *Straight Lick: The Cinema of Oscar Micheaux*. Bloomington and Indianapolis: Indiana UP, 2000.

Kawash, Samira. *Dislocating the Color Line: Identity, Hybridity, and Singularity in African-American Literature*. Stanford: Stanford UP, 1997.

Keller, Frances Richardson. *An American Crusade: The Life of Charles Waddell Chesnutt*. Provo: Brigham Young UP, 1978.

Lewis, David Levering. *W.E.B. Du Bois, 1868–1919*. New York: Holt, 1993.

Rocchio, Vincent F. *Reel Racism: Confronting Hollywood's Construction of Afro-American Culture*. Boulder: Westview, 2000.

Sundquist, Eric J. *To Wake the Nations: Race in the Making of American Literature*. Cambridge: Harvard UP, 1993.

Wyatt-Brown, Bertram. *Southern Honor: Ethics and Behavior in the Old South*. New York: Oxford UP, 1982.

Performing Race

Mixed-Race Characters in the Novels of Charles Chesnutt

KEITH BYERMAN

Under the old code noir of Louisiana, the descendant of a white and a quadroon was white. Under these laws many persons currently known as "colored" or, more recently as "Negro," would be legally white if they chose to claim and exercise the privilege. . . . In South Carolina, the line of cleavage was left somewhat indefinite; the color line was drawn tentatively at one-fourth of Negro blood, but this was not held conclusive. "The term 'mulatto,'" said the Supreme Court of that state in a reported case, "is not invariably applicable to every admixture of African blood with the European, nor is one having all the features of a white to be ranked with the degraded class designated by the laws of the State as persons of color, because of some remote taint of the Negro race. . . . The question whether persons are colored or white, where color or feature is doubtful, is for the jury to determine by reputation, by reception into society, and by their exercises of the privileges of a white man, as well as by admixture of blood.

—CHESNUTT, "The Future American"

The passage above, from Chesnutt's 1900 article "The Future American," offers a legal (and legalistic) description of race that dovetails nicely with current discussions of that concept as a social construction. In this sense, it is also clearly relevant to a discussion of *House behind the Cedars,* published the same year as the essay, as well as *Paul Marchand,* written twenty years later. What I believe interested Chesnutt in these stipulations of racial identity is what might be called their reasoned arbitrariness. One's status, with regard to legal restrictions and privileges, varied by state, time period, and, in the case of South Carolina, by reputation. These rules were in place at the very time that the assertion was being made both socially and "scientifically" that "race" was an absolute and fixed biological category. What I wish to suggest in my discussion is that the two novels above might be considered as thought experiments by Chesnutt that track the meaning of such arbitrariness. In this sense, I am interested in the performance of race in these works rather than in the nature of its reality. My analysis is in large measure a dialogue with SallyAnn Ferguson and Dean McWilliams, whose engagement with the issue of mixed-race representation in Chesnutt is long-standing and substantial.[1]

In "The Future American," Chesnutt argues for amalgamation as the solution to America's racial problems. He sees it, from a logical and scientific viewpoint, as an easy means of ending racism and creating a vibrant future. Ferguson and McWilliams have pointed out the substantial flaws in his thinking, both as rhetorical gesture and as racial commitment.[2] What I would suggest is that such "flaws" are calculated acts of provocation designed to discomfort the audience rather than persuade it. Since Chesnutt contends, early in the article, that race is a fiction and that the states have long recognized it as such in the laws they have constructed, he chooses to foreground this reality and, perhaps somewhat facetiously, turn it into a national virtue. It is unclear whether Chesnutt intended the article to be taken seriously as a proposition. For example, he notes the popular expectations for a new "American race":

This perfection of type—for no good American could for a moment doubt that it will be as perfect as everything else American—is to be brought about by a combination of all the best characteristics of the different European races, and the elimination, by some strange alchemy, of all their undesirable traits—for even a good American will admit that European races, now and then, have some undesirable traits when they first come over. It is a beautiful, a hopeful, and to the eye of faith, a thrilling prospect. The defect of the argument, however, lies in the incompleteness of its premises, and its obliviousness of certain facts of human nature and human history. (96)

The humor of the passage, in its parody of American progressivist language, suggests the difficulty of achieving the goal of homogeneity within the "white" race alone. Clearly, he understands the much greater difficulty of mixing groups separated by generations of social, legal, and ideological oppression and physical violence used to maintain that oppressive order.

At the same time, he knows that modern science has demonstrated the falseness of race as a biological category. For him, it makes no sense to continue to believe in something so absurd. He also demonstrates, through a variety of examples, the reality of racial mixing, a historical situation that necessitates the laws described at the beginning of this essay. "There are no natural barriers to such an amalgamation. The unity of the [human] race is not only conceded but demonstrated by actual crossing" (97).

The article can be best understood, then, not as an actual proposal for social change that would occur by choice within a relatively short period of time, but rather as a hypothesis that carries science and social practice to a logical end. "Amalgamation" is already occurring, despite segregation and miscegenation laws; there are no biological barriers to it; human beings are, in fact, already one race; and there is in place popular acceptance of some form of ethnic mixing. What if, then, instead of resisting this natural and inevitable process, Americans embraced it? The outcome, in Chesnutt's view, would be the resolution of an otherwise intractable problem. The article offers little indication that the society will actually do something so reasonable.

What does this stance mean for the fiction? It seems to mean that the two novels under discussion here (as well as some of the short stories) are mechanisms by which Chesnutt explores the implications of the fiction of race as a "natural," biological category of human difference. This approach, I believe, might help to elucidate some of the problems of the texts by suggesting their usefulness in conducting the experiments and their status as markers of arbitrariness. Two examples of such problems are the extensive reliance on coincidence to advance the plot of *House behind the Cedars* and the long-term concealment from Paul Marchand of his parentage, a secret which repeatedly subjects him to racial insult.

The story of *House behind the Cedars* simply could not be told without the use of plot devices that either separate or bring together characters at crucial moments. Among other instances, Rena and George end up in Patesville at the same time, George's relative is Molly's doctor, Judge Straight is advisor to both families, letters get misdirected or ignored, Rena ends up teaching in George's neighborhood, George and Wain approach Rena along converging paths, leaving her only escape into the swamp as a storm breaks. While such tricks of plot are common to romance, they are not generally so prevalent in what is considered to be realistic narrative.

Such textual manipulation suggests that the characters and story alone would not produce the conflicts and possible resolutions that Chesnutt wants to consider, despite Ferguson's claim that Rena is the product of his sexist projections ("Rena" xx).[3] Given the artificiality of racial difference, as we shall see, not even his theme of reason and sentiment, so essential to characterization, can quite work. The problem starts with the law. As a child, John walks into Judge Straight's office and declares that he wants to become a lawyer. When the judge reminds him of the "social disability" of his race, John declares himself white, based on the empirical evidence of his physical appearance. They then examine the laws on racial identity, with the Judge quoting the passage from the South Carolina courts cited above. What he also notes is that, by North Carolina law, John is probably far enough removed from black ancestors to be "white." In other words, his black identity becomes a matter of consent rather than descent, to use Werner Sollors' terms.[4] John is in a position to choose his racial identity and does so to personal advantage and with the judge's tacit approval, effectively undermining any meaningful essentialist argument.

Once he establishes himself as a lawyer in South Carolina,[5] John is legally a white man, by both ancestry and reputation. And his performance of whiteness is highly successful; he shows command of "white" discourse so well that his sarcasm about social and racial matters is taken as a sign of his breeding. Having made what he considers a rational decision to be white, he cannot really be thought of as "passing,"[6] since the law recognizes his status as legitimate. If the novel is an experiment, then John makes one kind of choice: to accept the identity available to him as an individual and not concern himself with biology or a racial past that was itself arbitrarily assigned.

What might be seen as his sentimental error, bringing Rena from her "black" home in Patesville to his world in South Carolina, only becomes a difficulty through plot manipulation. After attending boarding school, she is brought into white society and is an instant success. At her first social event, she is selected as the Queen of Love and Beauty and enthralls George Tryon. Like her brother, she successfully crosses the color line through her performance of whiteness. Even her self-consciousness is taken as evidence of her white Southern womanhood. But, unlike her brother, she might be said to be "passing" in the sense that she seems to accept the one-drop rule about race. Despite what the law and opportunity say, she troubles herself about whether to reveal her ancestry to Tryon, and she continues to feel a connection to her old home as both domestic and racial space.[7]

But I would argue that her position, in the context of the novel, is as arbitrary as any other. Her mother, Molly, has little use for blacks and wishes her daughter to marry as light as possible. Rena's own position is one of condescension. Her weakness is her sentimentality, but it is not the source of her tragedy. Her belief in dreams and her homesickness lead her back to Patesville, but without authorial interference, she could return to her brother's home with her mother's blessing. Molly, who idolizes the memory of the man who fathered her children, could want nothing better than to have a marriage to Tryon, even if it meant virtually never seeing her daughter again. After all, she does not seem to have suffered from the loss of her son, and she willingly sends Rena off with Jeff Wain, whom she misreads as a wealthy, powerful, and light-skinned potential husband. It can also be contended that Rena functions more successfully as a white woman than as a black one, precisely because the color of her skin creates a variety of problems she is not equipped to handle. In terms of the experiment, Rena's different approach could lead to the same result as John's.

In other words, the narrative problem here is generating substantial conflict over racial identity. Given what he sees as the falsehood of racial difference, Chesnutt finds it relatively easy to create black characters that are moral, intelligent, and socially adept. They can, without difficulty, move into mainstream American culture as long as skin color can be ignored. When it cannot, as in the case of Frank Fowler,[8] they can still be the noblest of the characters. So the question becomes how to complicate the narrative so that there is at least the appearance of a problem. The solution in this novel is to create a series of coincidences that expose the "secret" and then keep the lovers separated so that they do not devise a solution. This makes it possible to expose Tryon's racism, but then necessitates undermining it in the name of love.

The "tragedy" that is the death of Rena, which could be said to be a "black" version of the tragic mulatto master narrative (in that it supposedly shows the unfairness of a race-obsessed society), can thus only occur through extravagant authorial intervention. I want to argue that Rena must die because there are too many ways to have her live happily ever after.[9] If she took her mother's or her brother's advice, if she could at least imagine her lover's change of heart, if she could give up her own essentialist notions, she could easily have the life her class position and physical appearance have made possible. In essence, Chesnutt can be said to see the real tragedy in her inability to be the "future American."

In *Paul Marchand*, the issue might be said to be reversed in that the protagonist has to engage the problem of *not* being black after all. He lives into young manhood quite successfully in the role of quadroon, acquiring wealth and status within the boundaries of that identity. He shares the attitudes of those in his group, including a strong link to French and Creole cultures. His pride and sense of self-worth unfortunately create problems for him, since some whites feel compelled to establish their superiority over him. Because they cannot do this through strength of character, they must do it through exploitation of racial rules of the society. This situation produces two effects in Paul: resentment of the humiliation he faces and an effort to acquire attributes associated with whites: possessions, reputation, skills (such as fencing), and culture. What is important is that he does not see this as imitating whites, but rather as claiming what ought to be his in any just society.

But Chesnutt is not interested in producing another narrative which simply points to the unfairness of racial discrimination. Paul Marchand looks white, has high moral character, pride, talent, everything that a racist society claims as the exclusive property of whites, yet he is denied the benefits of his virtues. For Chesnutt, all that is obvious. The interesting question here is what would happen if he were, in fact, white. In effect, the author reverses the situation of "Mars Jeem's Nightmare," which was intended to show whites what life was like on the other side of the color line. In that instance, the differences between the races are taken as absolute; one is either black or white. In the novel, there is a character who is already on the color line (he can, for example, get into the quadroon ball by acting like a white man) and then crosses over into an apparently fixed identity.

Paul Marchand is a narrative filled with performances of whiteness. It opens with Zabet, a "mahogany brown" woman who had once been "young and fair and slender," who is taken as a quaint and entertaining relic of New Orleans, but who, in fact, is the spy and agent of Pierre Beaurepas. One key is her mastery of languages: when the occasion calls for it, she speaks "excellent" French, Creole, or "Negro French." She also plays the role of free black, though there is no evidence of free papers.

In addition, she is the mechanism by which Chesnutt sets the main plotline in motion, as she tells each of the Beaurepas cousins that their dying uncle would be happy to have them visit him as part of the patriarch's scheme about inheritance. Each of the cousins (with the exception perhaps of Phillipe) then adopts the role of worthy heir in meeting with their uncle. But more than this performance, I would argue that each of them performs his whiteness with regard to the putative quadroon Paul Marchand. Paul keeps a small book in which he records offenses against himself, especially by the cousins. While such insults would not be uncommon in the racial environment of New Orleans (or any other Southern space at the time), Chesnutt is careful to point out that each insult, in fact, violates the accepted behavior of Creole gentlemen. Through the comments of observers, he points out that Henri, Hector, and Raoul are either at fault themselves or behave inappropriately in their encounters with Paul. And, though we do not see Adolphe's offense, he is later proven a coward. Thus, each man, in "acting" white, exceeds the role. Such excess suggests an anxiety of whiteness, especially since it involves the all-but-white Paul Marchand. They must each overplay their part because otherwise Paul's clear superiority in everything except skin color will be obvious to everyone, including themselves.

But, of course, this is precisely the joke of the text, since Paul is, in reality, white by ancestry. This plot twist also has implications for the performance of whiteness, involving as it does the source of his racial identity (his parents) and his own actions during the short time he lives as a specifically white man. Dean McWilliams has explored at length the issue of concealing Paul's identity (182–207). Certainly, Pierre Beaurepas's withholding of the information and his lawyer's participation in the deception raise significant questions about the morality and humanity of these characters. What parent would allow his child to endure the affronts Paul must suffer?

But this moral issue is secondary when we consider the text as thought experiment. One effect of this plotline is to allow Paul to experience life on the color line, with particular emphasis on the arbitrariness of that line. In France, we are told, he has no specific racial identity; he does not endure insults based on his presumed parentage. In this text, instead of using the conjuring device of "Mars Jeem's Nightmare," Chesnutt uses the supposedly more realistic device of a family secret. The problems that McWilliams raises about the device, perhaps, are ways it exposes itself as a device (196–200). As in the short story, it serves as a means of letting a white man see the meaning of blackness, but I believe that Chesnutt here takes the idea even further.

After Mars Jeem goes through his experience as a slave and returns to whiteness, he is transformed to the extent that he gets rid of the overseer and becomes known as the kindest master around. As a result, he wins the hand of a worthy woman and lives happily ever after. In Paul Marchand-Beaurepas's case, he actually tries out the power of whiteness. He challenges the cousins to duels as a matter of honor. He defeats each of them in a manner symbolically appropriate to the insult he suffered. In the duel with the cousins, Paul "accidently" cuts Raoul in the very spot on the face where Raoul had slapped him in public. Henri, who had been responsible for ejecting Paul from the quadroon ball, is cut on the thigh and, according to the doctor, "will not be able to dance for a month or six weeks" (113). He pretends initially that his strikes against them are accidents, the result of his "black" upbringing, but they quickly realize the truth of his superiority. In both the pretense and the actuality, he demonstrates the cold-bloodedness and calculation that the text repeatedly associates with whites.

In a scene that McWilliams finds especially troubling (193–194), Paul threatens Zabet with violence and re-enslavement unless she gives him the other family secret, the name of the cousin who is, in fact, not white. While we are not told directly the answer, it is obvious that that person is Philippe. When Paul gives up his claim to the estate and names Philippe as the heir, he simultaneously and consciously "blackens" the family (from an essentialist perspective) and "whitens" Philippe, as well as giving him the woman he loves. Marchand, in other words, exercises a white man's prerogative of deciding the meaning of race.

What I would suggest about all these instances is that they allow Marchand to "try out" whiteness as an identity. He in effect learns the power that can be used with a recognized racial role. He can destroy and enhance lives, not based on character or achievement, but simply on the basis of skin color. And such power can come to him with a word. But what he also learns is that whiteness is always excessive, it always over-reaches itself. It leads him to violence, deceit, and revenge, qualities not high on the list of a civilized society.

He repudiates whiteness in the name of love and self-respect. One thing he cannot control as a white man is his marriage to Julie; the code noir that says that a white man cannot be legitimately married to a quadroon. This is the Law of the

Father, more powerful than any single white man. So he chooses Julie and France, not as a quadroon but as a man outside of the racial drama that is America.

In emphasizing the role of performance in these works, I would suggest that Chesnutt was engaging in speculation about a future nation. What if race were acknowledged as the false signifier he knew it to be, whether the science of the time could prove it or not? To go there, he had to think about whiteness and not merely blackness as a social construction. He chose to make whiteness in these works a performance and not a natural condition. John Walden could adopt the role of a white man and be accepted in that role based on the arbitrary marker of his skin color. His rejection of essentialist notions of race and social rules allow him to do precisely that. His sister, in contrast, must be made something of a fool *and* be the victim of authorial intrusion in order not to succeed in the racial role she so obviously fills. Paul Marchand is so clearly superior to those around him that the sudden change in his racial identity simply gives him a public opportunity to display his advantage. Having done so, he plays one last joke on white supremacy and then moves outside the quagmire of American racial politics altogether.

What Chesnutt finally suggests then, I would argue, is not that race might soon disappear as a social reality, but rather that that reality is based on irrational and silly assumptions. It can only be maintained by ridiculous (and violent) contrivances. His project in such a situation is not just to contend politically and socially against social conditions, but, as an artist, to point to the racial absurdity through his art.

Notes

1. See Ferguson, "Chesnutt's Genuine Blacks" and "Rena Walden"; McWilliams; Knadler; and Watson.
2. See McWilliams; and Ferguson, "Chesnutt's Genuine Blacks."
3. I do not particularly disagree with Ferguson's point, but wish to suggest an alternative reading of its implications.
4. See Sollors, *Neither Black nor White*.
5. Chesnutt must have found special irony in being able to use as John's "white" home the first state of the Confederacy precisely because of its flexibility in defining race.
6. For discussions of passing, especially in Chesnutt's work, see Sollors, *Neither Black nor White;* Sheehy; and Callahan.
7. See Ferguson, "Rena Walden," on this point.
8. On a different reading of this character, see Ferguson's essay on Fowler. SallyAnn Ferguson, "Frank Fowler: A Chesnutt Racial Pun," *South Atlantic Review* 50.2 (1985): 46–53.
9. For different readings of Rena and the novel more generally, see McWilliams, 53, 132–146; and Ferguson, "Rena Walden."

WORKS CITED

Callahan, Cynthia A. "The Confounding Problem of Race: Passing and Adoption in Charles Chesnutt's *The Quarry*." *Modern Fiction Studies* 48.2 (2002): 314–340.

Chesnutt, Charles. "The Future American." 1900; *MELUS* 15.3 (1988): 95–107.

———. *House behind the Cedars*. 1900; New York: Macmillan, 1969.

———. *Paul Marchand, F.M.C.* Jackson: UP of Mississippi, 1998.

Ferguson, SallyAnn. "Chesnutt's Genuine Blacks and Future Americans." *MELUS* 15.3 (1988): 109–119.

———. "Rena Walden: Chesnutt's Failed Future American." *Southern Literary Journal* 15.1 (1982): 74–82.

Knadler, Stephen P. "Untragic Mulatto: Charles Chesnutt and the Discourse of Whiteness." *American Literary History* 8.3 (1996): 426–448.

McWilliams, Dean. *Charles W. Chesnutt and the Fictions of Race*. Athens: U of Georgia P, 2002.

Sheehy, John "The Mirror and the Veil: The Passing Novel and the Quest for American Racial Identity." *African American Review* 33.3 (1999): 401–415.

Sollors, Werner. *Beyond Ethnicity: Consent and Descent in American Culture*. New York: Oxford UP, 1986.

———. *Neither Black nor White yet Both: Thematic Explorations of Interracial Literature*. Cambridge: Harvard UP, 1997.

Watson, Reginald. "The Tragic Mulatto Image in Charles Chesnutt's *The House behind the Cedars* and Nella's Larsen's *Passing*." *CLA Journal* 46.1 (2002): 48–71.

A Question of Passing or a Question of Conscience

Toward Resolving the Ending of Mandy Oxendine

Donald B. Gibson

Many who have written about Charles Chesnutt's first known novel, *Mandy Oxendine*, unpublished during the author's lifetime, have discussed its ending, an ending somewhat problematical because it invites the reader to speculate about what happens to its main characters after the novel's close. The narrator, who could know and tell us what happens, had Chesnutt chosen to allow him to do so, simply does not say. Rather he gives us alternatives about what might have happened, refusing to provide any certainties relating to Tom Lowrey and Mandy's future. Chesnutt does, however, control the character and direction of what we do *not* know. He might, for example, have ended the narrative, "Whether Tom died in a railroad accident and Mandy became a wealthy landowner pursued by a bevy of suitors, I cannot say." But he does not do that. He chooses, instead, to raise the question about whether they pass for white at the end of the novel: "Whether they went to the North . . . or whether they chose to sink their past in the gulf of oblivion, and sought in the great white world such a place as their talents and their virtues merited, is not for this chronicle to relate" (112).[1] I do not think the reader would have anything to say in support or denial of Tom's dying in a railroad accident, but do I think there is a great deal to say about whether Tom and Mandy decide to pass after the ending of the novel. I would go so far as to say that I can build a case around the question—one that proves that they *do not* pass. The matter is worth pursuing; in fact, Chesnutt invites us to do so throughout the narrative, offering the reader enough evidence to make a meaningful evaluation of the question. I think Chesnutt made an emphatic stance against passing in this novel in large part by setting forth the possible fates of Mandy and Tom in regard to their passing for white, inviting the reader to share that conclusion. The novel is, at its center, a cautionary tale that strongly warns of the pitfalls and dangers of passing. It gives us examples of people who could easily pass if they chose to but whose experiences and consciences countermand any such temptation.[2]

Though the novel is named after Mandy Oxendine, and Mandy is the novel's center of focus, Tom more nearly reflects the novel's center of values since his principles are more closely aligned with the narrator's, and his character is drawn in such a way as to establish a standard of thought and behavior supported and approved by Chesnutt and filtered through the novel's narrator. Still, although Tom's perspective is closer to that of the author than to any other characters in the novel, the narrator and Tom can be differentiated. There are things that happen in the narrative that Tom is not aware of and cannot know because he has no means of knowing (for example, Mandy's interaction with her mother). There are also moments in the narrative when Tom's attitudes and opinions are called into question and when his perspective is not reliable, as in his inability to see Mandy objectively. At other times, the narrator is free of the constraints binding the characters under his and the author's control and is privy to information unavailable to Tom, including access to the thoughts of other characters. Throughout the course of reading and thinking about this novel, the reader must be ever sensitive to the relations between Tom, the other characters, and the narrator in an effort to determine whether the author agrees with, disagrees with, or is ambivalent about Tom's thoughts, attitudes, and judgments. Doing so allows us to better understand the narrator's (and, therefore, Chesnutt's) intentions concerning our reading of the text.

It is clear, for example, that the beginning of the novel finds Tom Lowrey and the narrator in complete accord in relation to their shared code of decency; he sets a standard of appearance, manner, and demeanor that applies to everyone else who will appear in this fictional context. Early in the novel, when Tom arrives in Rosinville, North Carolina, ready to assume a teaching position in the "school for colored children" (9), Tom spots the man he assumes is at the train station to meet him. Though Tom has no firsthand knowledge of the person who will meet him, he is expecting to find a person lower in social station than himself, so he looks "among the porters and loiterers about the depot, and finally [directs] his steps toward an elderly 'negro,' who had walked along the side of the passenger coaches and was now standing near the door of one of them, looking around in evident perplexity" (4).

Tom's sense of his relation to this "negro" allows him to approach him in a direct and undisguised manner and to confront him with a question, "Are you looking for someone?" To Tom's query, the African American man answers Tom, "Yas, boss, I wuz a-lookin' fer a young colored man what wuz comin' in de kyars" (4). The assumptions of each character concerning the other are confirmed in the ensuing interchange between them even as the apparently accepted hierarchical relationship, based in large part on appearances, unfolds: Tom wears a suit and appears to be white and Deacon Pate, the man Tom confronts, is black. In addition, their different levels of education, made obvious by Mr. Pate's dialect and Tom's use of standard English, would necessarily result in Deacon Pate's deference to Tom regardless of his perceived racial identity. And how, one might ask, is the narrator seeing this meeting between Tom and Mr. Pate? Tom is without doubt "respectful," but in a condescending way, and the narrator views Tom's relation with Deacon Pate as perfectly natural. Despite Tom's civil inter-action with Deacon Pate, Tom is, from his own and the narrator's perspective, Pate's superior. As readers we might or might not agree that their differing social circumstances allow one to be superior to the other, but, nonetheless, the text asserts the character of their relation.

The narrator continues to underline the disparity between Tom and Deacon Pate's social relationship established in their first encounter. Note the compara-tive dignity of the two during the course of their exit from town.

Mr. Pate untied the mule, took the rope lines in his hands, and perched himself on one side of the cart, his feet dangling down. Lowrey took a similar position on the other side, and put up his umbrella to keep off the sun. (5)

I do not mean to be unduly critical of the narrator (nor of Chesnutt, ultimately, since this narrator is usually totally reliable) so much as to describe what is in the text. The lack of distance between the narrator and the character, Tom, allows the reader better to understand what Chesnutt wants to tell us.

Tom's further interactions with the deacon serve as precursors to help reflect and define his relations with other black people in the town. The reader learns a great deal about how we are to regard Deacon Pate and the other black denizens of Rosinville after the following observation rendered by Pate:

"Chu'ch begins at half pas' nine, Brer Lowry," said the deacon, picking his teeth with a jack-knife as they rose from the table. [Tom, of course, would *never* pick his teeth with a jack-knife.] "I reckon a little religion'll go good on top er dat chicken. 'Pears ter me de Lawd 'ain' done so bad by the cullud folks after all. He made 'em po' and black, but he give 'em religion an' chickens, de two things dey 'preciates mos'." (9)

This self-mockery, relying as it does on the ubiquitous stereotype of the chick-en-stealing slave, is apparently intended for the amusement of Chesnutt's white readers. (It is apparent that Chesnutt did, indeed, write for a white audience—for people whose racial attitudes he hoped to influence.)[3] Other elements of the novel are also intended to make such an appeal. When "Brer Lowrey" is intro-duced to "Brer Scott," the narrator indirectly tells us that the introduction fol-lows a formula with Lowrey being asked finally, "How's all yo' folks?" This seems humorous since neither knows anything of the other's family, but it becomes more significant if we are aware that in several west African languages part of a greeting ritual requires each party to inquire into the well-being of the other's family. Chesnutt, himself not recognizing the ritual nature of the question, and being outside that circle of racial and cultural awareness and interaction, readily treats it as humorous for Lowrey and for his reading audience.

One cannot help but recognize the differences between Tom's speech and Brother Pate's and the other members of his community.[4] The successful attempt is made to distinguish between the two "languages," the end being to establish the one as more valuable, meaningful, correct, and significant than the other. One is a standard language, the other vernacular. And the distinction to be made is by no means intended to establish racial distinction only, but class distinction as well. The whites who participate in the final scenes of the novel, during which Tom is going to be lynched for allegedly killing the white seducer of Mandy, Robert Utley, are not necessarily presented as either better or worse than the common, ordinary people who exist in the world of Brother Pate: the connection between both communities lies in the fact that their language marks them as social inferiors. One white citizen, Dan Peebles, who tries to prevent the lynching of Tom, is morally superior to those who want simply to lynch any black person available; still, he is Tom's social inferior, and his language marks him as such. A distinction is made among the white participants of the lynch party in the following dialogue.

"I dunno," said Skinner stubbornly. "Pears like a pity ter buy this rope an' break our night's res' fer nuthin'. It's true the nigger didn't kill Utley, but he said he did, an' it kind er goes ag'in the grain fer me ter hear a nigger even *say* he killed a white man."

"*Don't* be so onpatient, Jeff." said Peebles. "We aint going ter hang the wrong man just to please you, even if he is a nigger. After all, he's a pretty white nigger. You kin save that rope; you may have a use fer it some other time."

"What's the matter," said a gruff voice from the outskirts of the Crowd, "with hangin' the preacher?"

"No, gentlemen," said Peebles with emphasis, "I purtest a'gin the si'gestion. Every man should have a fair trial and have his guilt passed on by a jury before he is convicted of a crime. The right to trial by jury is one of the bull-works of our libbutty." (110)

The point is not that people who speak non-standard English are simply dismissed. Here a meaningful distinction is made among people who speak the same underclass dialect. The difference between the values of those who want to lynch Lowrey and those who are obviously present but who do not speak is a very important difference. The weight of the textual meaning of those who support the voice that argues against lawlessness is significant. Yet there prevails the sense that those who speak a non-standard, colloquial dialect are not quite equal to those who speak standard English, and the latter see things more accurately and clearly. There is some limitation (as reflected in our inclination to smile) in one who speaks of "the bull-works of our libbutty": the humor, of course, lies not in the meaning of the words themselves, for they are heavily weighted and fraught with meaning in this context, but in their pronunciation. And, again, so much of what transpires in Tom Lowrey's classroom has to do with language proficiency, although Tom's perceptions based on physical appearance come into question in this setting. When Tom asks "the little black girl he had met at the spring" (on the day he came into town) her name, she replies in such a way as to indicate her inability to respond in adequate language to the simplest question, "What is your name?" She replies, "Mississippi Nova Scotia Rose Amelia Sunday." The narrator goes on to say, "She delivered this incongruous string of names in a rapid monotone so droll that it required an effort on Lowrey's part to repress a smile.

"Say it all over again," he said gravely, "and say it slowly so that I can take it all in."
She repeated her name.
"Is that all?"
"Dat's all, suh. I had some mo', but t'other teacher said dat was all he could git on one line in de roll-book; so I done forgot de res'."
"And what do they call you at home?"
"Dey calls me 'Shug'."
"Short for 'Sugar.' Well, I'll call you Rose Amelia."
"Yes, suh. 'Rose 'Melia Sunday'–is dat w'at my name gwine be?"
"Yes, I'll write it—'Rose Amelia Sunday.'" (15)

This dialogic interlude is intended to be comic, even to the point of minstrelsy.[5] The relationship between teacher and student is not simply that; there is some element of racial and class hierarchy as well. Part of the name Rose Amelia ascribes to herself seems ludicrous—"Mississippi Nova Scotia"—and only the portion of her name selected by Lowrey, Rose Amelia Sunday, becomes her official name, as Tom's documenting it in the roll book certifies. But turning back to Tom's first meeting with Rose Amelia, when he is introduced to her at the town spring, nothing about her is ugly or comical. She seems, instead, dignified and graceful as the following passage reflects:

Ere they [Tom and Deacon Pate] reached the branch . . . they passed a wayside spring from which a little negro girl with a yellow gourd was dipping water into a piggin. She looked up with lively curiosity as the cart approached.
"Hoddy, Unker Isaac," she said to the old man, meantime casting sidelong glances at the stranger.

"Hoddy, chile," replied the elder. "How's yo' mammy?"

"She's well. How's all yo' folks?" said the girl as she deftly lifted the piggin to her bare head.

"Dey all tol'able. Dis is yo' new teacher, chile. Make him yo' bes' bow." She stood erect, straight as an arrow, with the piggin balanced on her crown, and dropped a low courtesy. (8)

How changed is her appearance as Tom's perspective on her shifts when she appears as his student in the classroom.

He was about to call up one of the older girls, when his eyes rested on a face he had seen before. It was that of the little black girl he had met at the spring on Saturday. She was neatly dressed in a clean homespun frock, her hair elaborately "corn-rolled," and sat just a short distance from the teacher, her black, bead-like eyes fixed intently upon him with an expression of mingled curiosity and admiration. . . . As she stood before him he was struck by the contrast between the old and wizened look of her ugly little face, with its gleaming eyes and the meager childish figure surmounted by it. She might have been a precocious child of ten or an older girl of stunted growth. This latter supposition was strengthened by the attitude in which she stood, with her shoulders thrown back at such an angle as to suggest a malformation of the spine. (14–15)

This seeming transformation is notable. Is there something threatening about Rose Amelia that Tom recognizes in this classroom setting that he failed to see earlier at the spring? What is he experiencing that causes his perception of the girl to change so radically? The answer to these questions may lie in the narrator's delineation of the classroom scene and the reader's growing apprehension of Tom's tendency to associate physical appearance and literacy with social class. The narrator explains that Tom questions Rose Amelia concerning "the books used and the classification and methods of instruction employed by his predecessor" but extracts no usable information. He then queries "another *intelligent looking* girl"; but, interestingly, for it undercuts Tom's apparent reliance on physical appearance as a marker of intelligence, he "could learn [nothing] he considered worthy of adoption" from either girl (15, emphasis added).[6] Tom's correlating of literacy, looks, and social class becomes more complicated in the following chapter when he conceives a way to reconnect with his former love interest, Mandy Oxendine, who is now living close to Rosinville. The reader is invited to see Mandy in a rather complex way when Tom meets her on the Lumberton Road. On one hand, we see a rather simple-minded girl who speaks vernacular, one who does not appear particularly bright and whose sense of values—whose character, upon close examination—leaves something to be desired. The level of her speech and education puts her in a class of people within the context of the novel who all, in the opinion of the narrator (as well as Chesnutt and Tom Lowrey, I would argue), are stationed somewhat below Tom, although she stands above some others. Her previous letters to Tom when he was away at school are painfully self-conscious and awkward, and they reflect a certain level of ignorance, as the following example attests.

Dear Tom:
I take my pen in han' to let you no that I am well an doin well and hope this will fine you the same. I got yor letter out of the postoffis yistiddy, and was glad to hear that you was well and doin' well. It is so lonesome sence you went away. Make 'ase' an git thru school an come back to your own true love. Mandy (30)

Of course, it is not necessary that this letter appear in the text of the novel: no element of plot hinges on its inclusion. It serves merely to characterize Mandy, and especially to contrast her level of education and sophistication with Lowrey's. Chesnutt need not have gone further than this letter to characterize Mandy, but he chooses to do so when he describes the postscript underlying her signature, "a heart, with a fancy scalloped border, and below that, as by an afterthought, this beautiful and brilliant couplet":

If you love me like I love you,
No nife can kutt our love in 2. (30)

Were there no indication from the narrator about how we are to read this letter and the accompanying poem, we might imagine that we are simply seeing it as it is and not judging it in a negative way, but, in fact, we are directed by the narrator to read the letter in a certain way (in case we have missed the earlier clues) when he refers to the couplet as "beautiful and brilliant." Obviously, it is neither "beautiful" nor "brilliant," and the narrator, without doubt, knows that. When we hear Mandy speak, her speech parallels the non-standard grammar and usage noted in her writing. Chesnutt intends that we see some relation between her language and her character as the narrator prompts us to do with other characters, including Tom. When Tom and Mandy's speech is juxtaposed during their conversation on the Lumberton Road, comparison between the two is obviously invited.

"You know why I went away [to attain a higher education]," he said, "and that it was for your sake I went. I wanted to learn something so I could be somebody, and give you a chance."

"Yes," she said, "an' you lef' me in the woods, 'mongs' niggers, and tu'pentine trees, an' snakes an' screech-owls. An' I got tired of 'em. . . . You lef' me 'mongs' niggers, an' I wouldn't be a nigger, fer God made me white," she added passionately, "an' I 'termined ter be what God made me, an' I *am* white. Nobody here knows anything different, an' nobody will unless you come here with your frien'ship and tell it." (23)

Immediately after this exchange—which turns out later in the narrative to be of great importance—the narrator speaks, giving voice to what Tom sees before him; and since the language of the narrator is indistinguishable from Tom's, the implication is that Tom's views are being expressed concomitantly with the narrator's.

She looked superb as she stood with an angry flush on her cheeks and an angry glitter in her eyes, declaring her independence, her revolt against iron custom. In her intensity of feeling she had drawn herself up to her full height, and the statuesque lines of a noble figure, unspoiled by the distorting devices of fashion, were visible through a frock whose scantiness lent but little envious drapery to conceal them. Her gingham sunbonnet had fallen back, disclosing a luxuriant head of nut-brown hair, with varying tints and golden gleams as the light fell on it at different angles. By intuition or inspiration, she had gathered it into a Greek knot, which brought out the contour of a head, small but perfectly proportioned.[7] Her eyes were gray, but looked almost black as they reflected her emotion. (23)

In answering Mandy's question to him about what he is doing in Sandy Run, Tom has indicated that he teaches at the school for "colored" children and will, thus, be identified as black. Her response to this indicates that his association with their shared race concludes their relationship.

"A person has got to be white or black in this worl', an' I ain't goin' to be black. An' black folks an' white folks don't go together. . . . I'd ruther die than be a nigger again," she said fiercely, "to be hated by black folks because I'm too white, and despised by white folks because I'm not white enough." (23)

Lowrey's response to Mandy's impassioned speech is a rebuke. He understands very well what Mandy chafes against, but he disapproves of her judgment of black people, reflecting his own sense, however qualified, of identification, of common cause with them.

"You talk," said Lowrey, "as though God didn't make black people."
    "He made 'em; an' he made 'em black an' ugly an' pore," [responded Mandy.]
    "That doesn't sound well from your lips," he said reproachfully." (23)

Tom's response that Mandy's words do not "sound well from [her] lips" reflects, first, on the disparity he feels between her words and her appearance. She is, in his view, beautiful; her words are ugly. The judgment is also a class judgment on his part: people identified with his ideal social station do not use the language Mandy does in speaking of race. I do not mean that Chesnutt did not share Mandy's sense of superiority to blacks, but I argue that his language and his class status are at one.[8] Such is not the case with Mandy. Her class aspirations and her language are, from the perspective of her author, at odds.

In the case of Robert Utley, Mandy's potential white lover, or, more correctly stated, seducer, Utley's class position and his morals are, from the author's perspective, also at odds, but the contradiction is not readily apparent. Although Utley uses standard English, he is unable, from the narrator/Chesnutt's viewpoint, to fulfill the moral obligations thrust upon him by his class standing: he is not, from Chesnutt's perspective, a "true gentleman." When Mandy tells Tom that she believes Utley is prepared to marry her, Tom reminds Mandy of the class hierarchy that will preclude Utley's doing so, despite her passing for white: "Who is the fine man . . . who will marry a sand-hill poor-white girl," Tom asks Mandy (24). Tom goes on to mock Mandy's belief that Utley will marry her and, thus, "make [her] a lady" only because Utley *says* that he will. Mandy responds, "You speak as if I belonged to you or you had some right over me." Tom replies simply, "I have the right every man has to protect a woman against a scoundrel" (24): Tom, the narrator, and Chesnutt are in concert on this point. We know at this point that Mandy is, indeed, being foolish, and that Tom, though his thinking is motivated by jealousy, is right about Utley's character. When the reader, then, considers Tom's ensuing foolish and uncharacteristic outburst in declaring his willingness to pass for white, he or she must do so in its full context.

"But come with me, and I will take you away, far away, and we will both be white. It was for you I went away to get learning, and for you I'd be white or black—or blue or green, if it would please you, sweetheart," he said, as he seized her hand, which was hanging by her side. . . . "I'll finish out my school," he said, "and I'll take the money, and we'll go away, and I'll work and study; and having a white man's chance, I'll make money, and you shall be a white lady." (24)

We should recall that this impassioned speech follows upon Tom's visualizing Mandy's naked body moments before: "the statuesque lines of a noble figure . . . . visible through a frock whose scantness lent but little envious drapery to conceal them" (23). We are called upon to account for Tom's seeming willingness to pass when he has before given us very sound and convincing reasons why he does not pass, why he has chosen to rise above the constraints levied against him by means of education, and how passing is not an option for him because of the moral implications of appearing to be different from what those he meets expect him to be. He feels it unfitting that he should mold himself to the expectations of others as passing requires.

We must, in other words, reconcile this assertion to Mandy that he will pass if she wishes it with his later description of his decision—made long before his meeting with Mandy on the Lumberton Road—not to pass. Before telling Mandy, in the heat of sexual desire, that he will pass for white if that is what it will take for her to consent to unite with him, he has decided and asserted that he will *not* pass.

But in spite of these disagreeable features of his position [for instance, white citizens mistaking him for a white and them blaming him when they discover their mistake], he had never felt the inclination to give up his people, and cast his lot with the ruling caste. His feelings were not entirely within his control, but his actions were, and there was something repugnant to him in the idea of concealment. (46)

At this point, the reader is confronted with two apparently different sets of values. The issue is not what we as readers think, but what the writer is thinking—what the novel says. How are we to respond to this apparent quandary? With whom do we agree, Mandy or Tom, considering each presents a different perspective on the issue of passing? The question as put to us by Chesnutt is finally whether passing is justifiable or even possible for people of conscience and sound morals. To understand the complexity of Mandy's decision to pass, the reader must learn more about her experiences and the development of her character as the narrative progresses. Ultimately, Tom and Mandy's dilemma is resolved by default. Once Mandy decides *not* to pass, as she does, contrary to the opinion of many readers, there is no longer an issue for Tom and, hence, no difficulty for him in reclaiming his moral stance on passing. It is not as though he has suddenly decided that passing is acceptable to him; on the contrary he has, in effect, said he will do whatever is necessary to possess Mandy, a pronouncement made in the intensity of its sexual overtones, as pointed out earlier. Tom concludes, "For you [Mandy] I'd be white or black—blue or green, if it would please you, sweetheart," words easily perceived as a "line" (24).

In furthering the case I am developing, it is worth noting that Mandy is presented as a lesser moral being than Tom, not in Tom's eyes but in the narrator's and author's. The narrator explains,

A woman's heart, like a weathercock, points steadily and true as long as the current of affection runs in one direction. But Mandy's feelings were in the variable state, now settling this way, and now that, as reason, recollection, ambition, passion, had each for the moment the upper hand. . . . If she had not met the other [Utley], it would have been a rise in the world to marry Tom Lowrey. (40–41)

In describing Mandy's vacillation between Utley and Tom, the narrator portrays Mandy as a whimsical opportunist, but the description of Mandy also reminds the reader that in the context of the novel, women, particularly black women, have no avenue for upward mobility except marriage. Mandy desires marriage to Utley because to Mandy "he represented that great, rich, powerful white world of which she dreamed, and to enter which since meeting him she had dared to aspire" (40). Mandy then decides on a seemingly failsafe course of action, a course stemming from the fact that she

was essentially human and essentially feminine. The upshot of her reflections was that she did not dislike Lowrey; that as men purely, she would scarcely know which to choose; that she would marry Utley, with his money and his position, if she could; but that she would hold Lowrey in reserve, and if Utley married his cousin [to whom he is engaged], she would take Lowrey, after making him do reasonable penance for his former neglect [his absence from her during the years of his education]. (41)

The narrator introduces his judgment of Mandy's decision and thereby indicates to the reader that equivocation between the two men has some significant limitations: "If she could have foreseen the result she might have hesitated before thus trying to carry water on both shoulders" (41). She is not utterly condemned by the narrator (nor the author), for the reader is led to believe Mandy's limitations stem not from immorality but from amorality, a function not of character but of gender, according to the narrator's description. Still, the narrator implies that Mandy is, by nature, incapable of achieving the same moral status as Tom. Even though her choice of Utley over Tom is rationalized, there still remains the disturbing note that her choice is motivated by speculation—by Utley's money, his higher status, and his ability to serve as her entrée to "the powerful white world." The fact that Tom is, as she states, "of her people," does not alter her thinking. She sees no harm in playing one man off against the other. Chesnutt presents this as an issue weighing heavily against Mandy. She seems incapable, at least initially, of considering the moral dimension of her actions.

Utley makes it somewhat plausible that Mandy might, with good reason and in good conscience, submit to his entreaties to marry him (because she erroneously imagines that he is actually offering that). She fails to see, in her naiveté, that the duplicity Utley exercises upon his creditors—pretending to marry his fiancée, "a rich girl," in order to obtain further credit—might be exercised upon her as readily. He tells Mandy,

"My engagement to a rich girl has enabled me to meet or renew obligations, to borrow money, to get on my feet, in other words. I can break it off now without utter ruin. It would make a scandal, I should be called a scoundrel, I should lose caste for a while. But, darling, what would all this amount to, weighed in the balance with your love?"

He whispered this softly into Mandy's ear. He had put his arm around her waist, against but faint resistance, and had drawn her close to him. She felt his breath upon her cheek. She doubted, and yet she listened. It sounded plausible, and yet so strange, so sweet, that a gentleman, white rich, handsome, ardent, should put himself in such a position for a poor girl such as she.

"Will you marry me, Mandy?" he said.

Through lips upon which he rained kisses, and with breath which was shortened by the pressure of his arms, she whispered, "Yes." (72)

The character of the dialogue between them is heavily influenced by their physical contact and by the sexual innuendo of their language and its subject. The conversation takes place at once on a sense and sensual level. Hence, when Utley challenges Mandy by asking whether he can trust her to carry through with her promise to marry him, Mandy's response, emerging from her unspoken yet underlying sense of duplicity in being engaged both to Utley and Tom, takes physical form.

"How can I prove it?" she said, unconsciously coming nearer to him and looking into his eyes.

He, responding in kind, drew her close to him.

"Give me the last, best proof," he whispered. "Be mine without reserve. Then I will know that you love me, and that you will not fail me." (73)

At this point, insight into the meaning of Utley's efforts causes Mandy to attempt to break away from him both physically and emotionally. "Mandy saw through his web of lies. She struggled to tear herself away from him, but he held her fast" (73). Though moments previously Mandy agreed to marry Utley, at this point she recognizes him as a vile seducer, and she obviously does not wish to pass at *any* price. As Utley struggles with Mandy, attempting to draw her deeper into the woods, with apparent intentions of raping her, "a dark form" appears, parts them, and ultimately kills Utley. From this moment on, Mandy is freed from the notion that she needs to be white, that her salvation lies in passing. The subduing and murder of Utley places her on another path of knowledge and understanding, redefines her sense of identity, and redirects the path of her life. We eventually learn that the "dark figure" who murders Utley is the white Reverend Gadson, who has, without Mandy's encouragement, become enamored of her; her "salvation" is a secular one brought about by the minister's jealous murder of the anti-Christ, Utley, whose horse is named "Satan." Utley's demise puts an end to Mandy's aspirations to move beyond her confined social state by marrying and passing into whiteness.

Mandy's attendance at Reverend Gadson's revival meetings, prior to Gadson's killing Utley, has prepared her for her conversion from her conviction that she needs to and can successfully pass for white to full integration of her self and with her culture. It also heightens the irony of Gadson's character and offers insight to Chesnutt's theme of appearance versus reality: Gadson is another white man who lusts after Mandy but whose religious zealotry has, prior to seeing her, precluded his delight in "earthly joys and sorrows" (53–54). In addition, he is a powerful rhetorician whose sermon brings Mandy to feelings of repentance and salvation, feelings that will allow her to align herself fully with her African American heritage. But Gadson is also a murderer whose initial cowardice in refusing to admit his guilt conveys, once again, the fissure between appearance (including language) and social status, truth, and conscience. Chesnutt goes to great lengths to convince us of the power of the minister and the awe he inspires in moving large numbers of people toward repentance and salvation. It is important that the reader witnesses Lowrey's emotional response to Gadson's preaching prior to Mandy's entering the scene: when Gadson sings a song in "an old fashioned wailing" voice, we grant that the congregation's combining their voices with the song generates a "weird volume of sound [that] floated out into the night and echoed far into the forest," a sound that produces in Lowrey "an almost indescribable melancholy" (49). Subsequently, "Lowrey was filled with strange emotions, and a sense of his own sinfulness oppressed him." As Gadson preaches, the narrator tells us that "John Wesley himself could not have described with greater detail their [the damned's] pangs and tortures" (50). The narrator describes,

Lowrey felt himself shiver and turn pale at the Dantesque particularity and gloom of the preacher's descriptions. It was uncanny, and he struggled to shake off the impression that pervaded him. He thought he would walk away into the woods for a moment until he recovered his mental equilibrium; but the sermon fascinated him. The preacher's eye seemed to pierce the gloom and fix itself upon him alone, and he could not move, as the anathema's of the preacher thundered around him. For a time he even forgot Mandy's presence and saw only the nightmare that had been conjured up. . . . He painted in tones of marvelous tenderness the love of Jesus, and the joys of paradise; and when the audience were sobbing like so many children, he towered to his full height and again invoked in harsh tones the wrath of God, and warned sinners to flee from it. (50)

Though it is clear from the tone of this passage, and Lowrey's response to it, that we are intended to read it as proof of the minister's effectiveness and his power, Lowrey himself notes that Gadson's "face was that of a man of strong passions, but of weak will," pointing out that the two faculties could combine for good or evil. The narrator elaborates that, thus far, Gadson's passion and will had "combined to work for the welfare of others" (48), intimating the imminence of the converse. At this point, the question arises, Will Mandy also be able to differentiate between the message and the messenger?

Once Mandy's presence at the camp meeting is made known to us, we take note that Gadson's rhetorical eminence profoundly affects Mandy; we recognize that Gadson has the power to put Mandy in a state of mind that allows her to see the incidents of her life against a broad background of religious and moral principles. Chesnutt is careful not to commit himself to the beliefs projected by Gadson while, at the same time, he allows his characters to be motivated by those projections. Hence the question of passing is moved to a higher level. And Mandy does see the difference between the message and the messenger, further enabling her to make the decision not to pass at the end of the novel. Unlike Lowrey, Gadson's sermon has moved Mandy to come up to the mourner's bench to profess her penitence and receive Reverend Gadson's prayers. However, instead of finding release and relief from her earlier "oppressing sense of sinfulness," she feels revulsion when the preacher places his hands on her head. The reader is made privy to Gadson's lustful feelings for the young, beautiful Mandy, the "odor of [whose] hair exhilarated him" as he "whisper[ed] words of encouragement" into her ear (53); and Mandy senses his passion for her and wants nothing more from him than to leave his presence. He will, however, reappear after Mandy confesses to the murder of Utley to complete his role in the advent of Mandy's reconnection with her race.

Mandy's transformation is advanced because of her initial belief that Tom is the murderer of Utley, and she decides that it is her duty to confess to the crime to protect him because of what she considers as her role and responsibility in it. The narrator leads the reader through Mandy's complete alteration, one that requires that she rethink her relationship with Tom.

She was innocent of the actual crime, for her hand had not struck the fatal blow. But was she not guilty before God? Had not this tragedy been the outcome of her own folly, her own lightness, her own wickedness? If so, was it not right that her life should pay the forfeit?. . . . The life of one she loved was in danger. For not until the murder had she realized how deeply, how passionately, how completely she loved Lowrey. There seemed to come back to her, in a great surge of feeling, the passion of two years before, when her heart first woke to love, when Tom was all the world to her . . . [and] everything would have seemed but dim phantoms, to be swept away as with a breath, if [anything] had stood between her and her love. . . . He had forfeited his life for her;

could she do less for him? In her present exalted state of mind life without him seemed not worth living. Life with him was now an impossible dream. Of what use to her in any event would be her life? She could not hope to conceal her antecedents longer, and she would not have cared to return to her old life. She made a grand resolve. (85)

That "grand resolve" is not only to sacrifice her life for Tom but also to become an acknowledged member of the black community; this decision stands in contrast to the decisions she has made heretofore—selfish, purely pragmatic decisions having to do with improving her living situation. She has been shaken to the very depths of her being and is no longer the superficial person whose life's meaning is determined by social circumstance. She repudiates the dictum that defined the most important consideration of her life, "I 'termined ter be what God made me, an' I *am* white" (23), tacitly transposing "I *am* black" for "I *am* white."

Ultimately, it is Reverend Gadson who helps bring Mandy's full transformation to light. Visiting Mandy in jail, Gadson tries to confess his guilt to her, arguing that it is not her sin but another's that brought her to her present predicament. She, however, insists,

"It was my own [sin that brought me here]. I was too proud to be what God made me, too vain to be content with my lot. I didn't act right, an' my punishment is just." (89)

It is obvious that Mandy now repudiates her previous rejection of her race, thus giving her a new found freedom. She refuses Gadson's entreaty to escape with him, marry him, and, thus, avoid execution. She tells Gadson that she does not love him and, consequently, marrying him would be a "livin' death" (90). At this point, the reader is convinced that Mandy has fulfilled her moral obligation to herself and her race, but is she a fully integrated woman? The answer is yes. In offering her life to save Tom's, Mandy shows that she is capable of complete devotion, the "currents of her affection" now run "in only one direction."

By the end of the novel, both Mandy and Tom escape the lynch rope (Tom, as willing as Mandy to sacrifice himself for love, falsely confesses to murdering Utley) when Reverend Gadson confesses to the murder. Tom and Mandy return to their hometown and are married, and the narrator informs us that they are "young enough to have much hope for the future, and much faith in themselves . . . and the gloom of their recent tragic experiences soon [wears] away" (112). These words, along with what Mandy has learned, with the help of two ignoble white men, and Tom has always believed in his heart—though he too was forced to look beyond the obvious for confirmation of his beliefs—corroborate that no option actually exists between their remaining "true to their own people" or "passing for white" in the North. The magnitude of their characters and the seriousness and importance of their recent experiences dictate the near impossibility of their willingly passing. Hence the question seemingly posed by the closing paragraph of the novel is no question at all. Of course they did not pass.

NOTES

1. This and other quotations are from Chesnutt's *Mandy Oxendine*.

2. Chesnutt himself superficially considered passing for white when he was in his teens. After being mistaken for white several times he states in his journal, "I believe I'll leave here [North Carolina] and pass anyhow, for I am as white as any of them [whites who presumed him white]," *The Journals of Charles W. Chesnutt*, 78. But, ultimately, as Charles Hackenberry (editor of *Mandy Oxendine*) points out, Chesnutt's "strong moral code would not allow him such equivocation" (xi).

3. For Chesnutt's sense of his audience and how he intended to influence them see William L. Andrews, *The Literary Career of Charles W. Chesnutt*, 13–16.

4. See Dean McWilliams, *Charles W. Chesnutt and the Fictions of Race*, 129–130, for a fuller discussion of the meaning of language differences as a characterizing factor in the novel.

5. See McWilliams, 127–128. McWilliams compares Rose Amelia to Topsy of Harriet Beecher Stowe's *Uncle Tom's Cabin*. Topsy, however, became a far more comic character in the later nineteenth-century minstrel productions of Stowe's novel than she was in the novel itself. Chesnutt's Rose Amelia does take on some of the characteristics of the minstrel figure.

6. One becomes more certain that Rose Amelia's appearance and her lack of intelligence are associated both by Tom and the narrator near the end of the novel when Rose Amelia, believing that her false report to her father has resulted in Tom's imminent lynching for the murder of Robert Utley, guiltily runs into the swamp and is later found dead. The narrator questions whether the death is a result of Rose Amelia's exhaustion or "whether in her remorse and despair she had taken her own life. . . . [but] her narrow brain, with the great passion it had yet been large enough to foster . . . had found rest from its throbbing" (106).

7. The reference to Mandy's tying her hair in a Greek knot could have implications for the reading of this passage (and of Mandy's character). The suggestion of Mandy's tying up her hair in a classical style does mitigate the sexual response that Tom has to Mandy, at least insofar as one perceives Mandy. Since loose hair has a long association with female sexuality in literature, Mandy's gathering up her hair undermines notions of any overt sexuality on her part. See Scott Gibson's chapter, "'They Were All Colored to the Life': Historicizing 'Whiteness' in *Evelyn's Husband*," in this collection for a thorough examination of Chesnutt's use of Greek allusions in relation to racial and ethnic implications at the turn of the nineteenth century, especially in association with the novel's titular heroine.

8. See Eugene D. Genovese, *Roll, Jordan Roll*, 437. Genovese writes about the relationship between social class and the use of the epithet: "Well-bred planters rarely used the word 'nigger' before the war, and their increasing use of it after the war provides one measure of their manner of experiencing the shock of emancipation. The yeomen used it more frequently and the poor whites almost invariably" (437). Genovese also notes that slaves themselves used the epithet frequently—the field hands more than the house slaves—and in doing so "destroyed its most poisonous effects and turned it to whatever advantage they could" (438). Mandy's use of the epithet may be more complicated than Tom allows if put in historical context.

Works Cited

Andrews, William L. *The Literary Career of Charles W. Chesnutt*. Baton Rouge: Louisiana State UP, 1980.

Chesnutt, Charles W. *The Journals of Charles W. Chesnutt*. Ed. Richard Brodhead. Durham: Duke UP, 1993.

———. *Mandy Oxendine*. Ed. Charles Hackenberry. Intro. William L. Andrews. Urbana and Chicago: U of Illinois P, 1997.

Genovese, Eugene D. *Roll, Jordan, Roll: The World the Slaves Made*. New York: Vintage, 1976.

McWilliams, Dean. *Charles W. Chesnutt and the Fictions of Race*. Athens: U of Georgia P, 2002.

"They Were All Colored to the Life"

Historicizing "Whiteness" in Evelyn's Husband

Scott Thomas Gibson

In his introduction to *Whiteness in the Novels of Charles W. Chesnutt*, Matthew Wilson asserts that Chesnutt "strove [in his writing] for a universal subject position that he perceived as outside of race" (xvii). Indeed, an aspiring Chesnutt refers to himself in his journal as an author who writes primarily "for the people with whom I am connected—for humanity!" (*Journals* xvii).[1] From the beginning of his career he had no interest in being pigeonholed as a "Negro" writer, which, in the eyes of the white literary establishment and his white readership, meant severe limitations on what was considered appropriate subject matter and style. Wilson and other critics refer to Chesnutt's acceptance speech upon receiving the Spingarn Medal in 1928, just four years before his death, as evidence that Chesnutt never gave up on this position. In this speech, Chesnutt claimed that he wrote "not primarily as a Negro writing about Negroes, but as a human being writing about other human beings" (*Essays* 514). It would be difficult to argue that he ever compromised this vision of writing for a common humanity, despite the failure of much of his work to affect social change. Unfortunately, his white critics and audience often received his writing with ambivalence and the perception that "race" alone was the appropriate topic for black writers, while reserving "universal" humanity for whites.

The issue of race is nonetheless an inextricable component of Chesnutt's writing and of American literature in general, as a result of the deeply ingrained racist legacy of the United States. Part of the failure among critics to recognize the pervasiveness of racial discourse has been the neglect of "whiteness" itself as a racial category, remaining complicit with its assumption of "universal" appeal. Recent interpretations of Chesnutt's work have drawn attention to his depiction of "whiteness," but they have also been limited by a theoretical lens contoured by the same distinction between nonracial "whiteness" and "racial" blackness that Chesnutt's white editors used to exclude his work from publication. This illogic, positioning unmarked "whiteness" in opposition to marked "race," reinforced by the heretofore unquestioned distinction between Chesnutt's "white-life" and "racial fiction,"[2] is not far removed from the racist thinking that eventually led to the consolidation of a homogenous, unmarked white identity and the "hardening of racial lines" in the first half of the twentieth century (Wilson x). My contention, and the subject of this chapter, is how to read *against* the grain of white racial identity in Chesnutt's *Evelyn's Husband,*[3] to show how this ostensibly "white-life" novel interrogates whites' claims to racial "superiority" and the "universality" of white experience, and how it creates spaces of overlap within and between sharp racial categories. This chapter will specifically show how *Evelyn's Husband* actively critiques white supremacists' redefinitions of white identity not only by suggesting "the possibility that whiteness could be changed and modified," as Wilson concludes (44), but also by critiquing the way whites *have already* "changed and modified" the definition of whiteness throughout modern history in order to maintain white power and the fiction of white racial purity.

The first step in understanding how *Evelyn's Husband* achieves this goal is to ask what whiteness meant in Chesnutt's time.[4] The short answer is that the definition of "whiteness" was in a constant state of flux due to the increasingly apparent heterogeneity of American demographics. For example, the American sociologist Peter Kivisto marks the years 1880 to 1924 as time when the second major wave of European immigrants entered the United States, reaching its peak in the early 1900s, when Chesnutt was working on *Evelyn's Husband.* The wave of immigrants was subsequently met with popular resistance and formal legislation to curb the massive influx of people, particularly those Europeans who were not unambiguously considered white, including the Irish, Jews, Slavs, and other European ethnicities. Identifying "race" as "the most powerful determinant shaping policies regarding citizenship," Kivisto argues that this new wave of immigrants forced Americans to redefine what it means to be an American citizen (44–45). Since full citizenship was theoretically democratic, but in practice restricted only to whites, part of this redefinition involved the "redrawing of the racial boundaries [that] resulted in the expansion of groups who were considered to be white" in the first half of the twentieth century (57–58). Kivisto specifically refers to the racial ambiguity of the Irish immigrants during this time, citing references to them as "white niggers" and the cartoon parodies by Thomas Nash that "portrayed [the Irish] as racially similar to Africans" (46). In this sense, to be "white" during Chesnutt's career was not just to have fair skin, but also to fit the very specific Anglo-American mold, a mold being shattered by the increasingly heterogeneous composition of the American population. Gradually, some of the "non-white" European ethnicities would become identified as white, and the dream of a "pure" white Anglo-American utopia would give way to a concessional (but equally racist) myth of a white European American nation. Both of these views, of course, excluded African Americans and other non-European decedents from full citizenship rights.

Not coincidentally, Chesnutt frequently attacked the Anglo-Saxon model of white racial purity by reminding white racists about the inherent diversity of the United States population. In "What Is a White Man?" for example, Chesnutt examines the "fiat" of the "wise men of the South" who claim the supremacy of the "all-pervading, all-conquering Anglo-Saxon race"[5] and the implications of this supposed birthright on claims to American citizenship (*Essays* 68). As whites sought to consolidate their power in the face of postbellum threats to their hegemony, Chesnutt demonstrated that such equivocation ignored the immense and increasing presence of people in the United States who did not fit this narrow definition:

It is not probable that he [Henry Woofin Grady] meant to exclude from full citizenship the Celts and Teutons and Gauls and Slavs who make up so large a proportion of our population; he hardly meant to exclude the Jews, for even the most ardent fire-eater would hardly venture to advocate the disfranchisement of the thrifty race whose mortgages cover so large a portion of Southern soil. What the eloquent gentleman really meant by this high-sounding phrase was simply the white race. (*Essays* 68)

Advocates of the "all-pervading, all-conquering Anglo-Saxon race," Chesnutt argues, are unaware of the slippery discourse of whiteness as it pertains to a nation of immigrants, whose ethnic and national backgrounds are more diverse than white supremacists are willing to admit. Chesnutt knew, however, that by assimilating all peoples of European descent into this broad fictional category of whiteness, the white supremacists at this time were creating the impression of a unified racial front that could further repress American blacks, who, just twenty years earlier, were granted the rights of citizenship under the Thirteenth, Fourteenth, and Fifteenth Amendments to the Constitution.[6] In *The Marrow of Tradition*, Chesnutt more specifically attributes this consolidation of white identity in the South to the fear of "nigger domination,"[7] which southern whites believed would occur if black Americans became the numerical majority in the United States or gained too much political and economic power.[8] The contradiction in white racial logic here is apparent: to protect "racial purity," the decreasing ratio of Anglo-Americans had to invent the fiction of a majority status by accepting more and more "impure" European ethnicities under the umbrella of whiteness.[9] In short, white supremacists were waging an ideological war on two racial fronts (against "non-white" immigrants and African Americans) by changing the definition of whiteness to suit their interests.

In *Evelyn's Husband,* Evelyn's "rich southern coloring—the belated inheritance of some distant ancestor"—seems to embody these same tense renegotiations of white identity because it represents how whites systematically included and excluded different people to maintain white power, privilege, and the fiction of white racial "purity" (25). Critics such as Ryan Simmons have noted that "the mere possibility of a presence of blackness in a prospective mate undercuts the logic by which the dominant class maintains its power" (52), a pattern which can be plainly seen throughout Chesnutt's fiction: for example, in George Tryon's rejection of the "mulatta" Rena Walden in *The House behind the Cedars.*[10] Under the guise of Romance, however, Chesnutt could not expect in *Evelyn's Husband* that a successful union between the "primitive" Hugh Manson and a "non-white" Evelyn Thayer would be acceptable to his readership, an assumption that has led critics to accept her "unquestioningly as white" (Simmons 53). Yet as Simmons notes, "It is hard to imagine . . . that this reference to the physical manifestation of Evelyn's heredity (and several other references to her dark complexion) is accidental" (52–53). Certainly, the "hints of these questions [of heredity]" that Chesnutt weaves into the novel are "not to be noticed except by the reader who has learned to look for them" (Simmons 55). While Chesnutt's white audiences would most likely have missed these hints, their significance in *Evelyn's Husband* becomes apparent when they are considered as part of his characteristic signifying strategy, the implications of which were consistently lost on his white readership.

Indeed, Chesnutt signifies on his white audiences throughout his works, most clearly in his "racial fiction." Comparing Chesnutt's signifying practices with Paul Laurence Dunbar, SallyAnn H. Ferguson argues that Chesnutt "grins and lies throughout his canon, knowing whites believed too deeply in their stereotypes of blacks—those testaments to their ignorance of and distance from African-American reality—to recognize the truth until he . . . had successfully accomplished some coup" ("Introduction" 11). Indeed, Chesnutt's fiction clearly illustrates his subversive literary finesse, as he tries to embed these scathing critiques within stories that, on the surface, appear benign. But if he could do this in his racial fiction, what precludes the possibility that he is also signifying in his white-life novels? Furthermore, if "whites believed too deeply in their stereotypes of blacks," did they not also implicitly stereotype their own racial identities?

Given the impact of European immigration on white identity at the time, one way to understand the way Chesnutt signifies in *Evelyn's Husband* is to connect Evelyn Thayer's "southern coloring" and irresistible physical features with the details of her southern European ancestry. During her first visit to the art museum, for example, Evelyn's courtier Hugh Manson comments on how Evelyn's "dark beauty" is set off by "a gown of clinging white" (15). Furthermore, he compares her beauty to Venus's, adding a cultural dimension to her physiological similarities with southern Europeans. To Manson, her appearance is the living inscription of an ancient artistic tradition. But Evelyn resists his flattery, and her response further contrasts her "dark beauty" with fair complexion: "That's a delightful compliment . . . [but] I had always thought of Venus as fair" (16). No such nuanced discussion of complexion in Chesnutt's work could be mere coincidence. As the discussion ensues, Manson complicates Evelyn's simple binary of "dark" and "fair" complexions by discussing the way the Venus statue's own whiteness has changed over time. He explains: "Because her [Venus's] statues are all of white marble? But they were all colored to the life, you must remember;—Greek art was faithful to nature. The Greeks were southern and dark" (16). Both "white" characters, Evelyn and Manson, like Chesnutt's readers, are unable to see the implications that her "dark beauty" and "southern coloring" might suggest the possibility of her non-white heritage. The narrator, however, leaves no doubt as to her dubious southern European ancestry: "Women of Evelyn's type were common in Italy and Spain, lands of love and languor" (17). Evelyn is clearly not the postbellum ideal of a purebred Anglo-Saxon Protestant woman; rather, she fits much more squarely into the various non-Anglo European (and potentially non-white) ethnic groups that were arriving in the United States in droves. Consequently, she represents the reality that all humans, even those who believe in the illusion of whiteness, are "colored to the life."

Furthermore, Manson's historically and culturally contextualized comparison between Evelyn's beauty and Greek art exposes a pattern of collective (and selective) historical amnesia among whites who sought to protect the myth of white racial purity as they faced constant reminders—embodied by African Americans, immigrants, and even their own physiological characteristics—that lay bare the fiction of their claims. While Evelyn naively imagines a "fair" Venus, Manson reminds her that Greek art (like Greeks themselves) was "colored," a term which conspicuously parallels the terminology Chesnutt often employed to describe light-skinned blacks. Like whites who ignore historical realities that would interfere with the fiction of white racial purity, Evelyn also assumes a legacy of consistently fair European ancestry that is reified through her image of Venus in the only way she has learned to view the statue: as uncolored white marble. Her interpretation of the statue's white appearance is clearly influenced by white supremacists' reconstructing whiteness as a historical and biological constant.

This trend of viewing Europeans and their American progeny as a historically homogeneous white racial group is further illustrated in *The Heart of Whiteness*, in which the author, Julian B. Carter, discusses how the "Norma" and "Normman" statues that appeared at the World's Fair in 1939 supposedly depicted an accurate representation of normal (white) Americans. According to Carter, these statues can be seen as the culmination of normalizing and universalizing of whiteness that began postbellum and extended well into the twentieth century, serving to define whites dialogically against blacks and to combat the perceived threat to white citizenship posed by non-white European immigrants. In contrast to the authentic Greek statue critiqued by Manson, the pale terracotta Norma and Normman make no pretensions of being "colored to the life"—they are unabashedly unpainted and uncolored representations of "normal" (white) Americans. In Carter's words, Norma and Normman represented "the ability to construct and teach white racial meaning *without appearing to do so*" (2). However, since the Greek statue in *Evelyn's Husband* has lost its coloring, it takes a specific knowledge of its having previously been colored to recognize that the museum, by displaying the bare white marble, is likewise participating in the whitening of history and culture in the white American imagination.

Chesnutt argued against this same process of homogenizing whiteness in his three-part "Future American" essay series just a few years before composing *Evelyn's Husband*.[11] Here Chesnutt explicitly sets out to discredit old theories of racial purity that have led to the "obliviousness of certain facts of human nature and human history" (qtd. in Ferguson, "Charles" 96). Turning to Professor William Zebina Ripley's 1899 study of *The Races of Europe*, Chesnutt bases his argument for the amalgamation of a future American ethnic type (consisting of a "predominantly white" mix of "white, black, and Indian" types) on scientific and historical evidence that "the secret of the progress of Europe has been found in racial heterogeneity, rather than in racial purity" (96–97). It should not be considered coincidence, then, that Manson dispels the same myth of the racially pure, fair-skinned European that Chesnutt rejected in his nonfiction just a few years earlier, or that is represented as a "normal" white American by Norma and Normman a generation later.

Evelyn, however, is certainly no "normal" white American woman. With her peculiar "dark beauty," Chesnutt portrays Evelyn in a sexualized manner that parallels descriptions of Chesnutt's "mulatta" characters, such as Rena Walden and Mandy Oxendine, in his racial fiction. In *Mandy Oxendine*,[12] for example, the title character is described as a woman with "no external evidence of Negro blood . . . unless a slight softening of facial outline, a dreaminess of eye, a mellowness of accent, might have been ascribed to its presence" (27). Rena Walden in *The House behind the Cedars* likewise passes for white with only subtle physical suggestions of her African ancestry. In this sense, *Evelyn's Husband* is no less subtle in its suggestion of racial amalgamation than Chesnutt's racial fiction. In fact, it becomes only a matter of critical perspective to see through the assumption of whiteness in *Evelyn's Husband* and acknowledge similarities in descriptive techniques across all three novels, thus further drawing into question the polarized categories of his racial fiction and white-life novels. If anything, Chesnutt goes to even greater lengths to describe the seductive features of Evelyn's dark beauty than he does his mulatta characters when he describes Edward Cushing's first impressions of her:

Cushing had lived too long, traveled too much, seen too many women in too many lands not to know the meaning of those slumberous, heavy-lidded eyes, those penciled brows, those full red lips, the firm, full contours of that perfectly moulded [*sic*] chin. Such eyes, clear and limpid now, were unsounded wells of feeling; such lips were made to give as well as to receive kisses. (16)

Conspicuously related to Cushing's travels around the world, this exoticized and eroticized description of Evelyn parallels (and perhaps even exceeds) the representation of white males' desire for mulatta women in Chesnutt's other fiction. The plots of the novels, too, suggest Chesnutt wanted to create some continuity between his white-life novels and his racial fiction. In particular, all three novels represent the women as objects of sexually motivated violence among their male counterparts. In *Mandy Oxendine*, for example, the degenerate aristocrat Robert Utley apparently tries to rape her before she is "rescued" by another admirer of hers, Reverend Gadson, who prevents the attack and kills Utley. In *The House behind the Cedars*, Tryon gives in to the "laws of nature"—presumably sexual desire—when he cannot rid Rena from his mind (148). His frenzied pursuit of Rena leads to her death when she tries to avoid him and her other equally base pursuer, mulatto character Jefferson Wain, both of whom try to accost her in a forest.

Described as a "naturalistic experiment" by Ryan Simmons, the battle between Hugh Manson and Edward Cushing for Evelyn's hand uses this same tension between "social convention" and human nature to understand the extent to which "civilized" white male characters will go to fulfill their desires if they can be freed from social limitation (46). In this way, all three novels echo Chesnutt's argument against miscegenation laws, which, as he points out, place the social convention of marrying within one's race in direct violation to the laws of nature; they also reflect his position, argued in "The Future American," that the success of European civilization is the direct result of racial heterogeneity among its people. It should be little surprise then that Evelyn Thayer's seductive beauty initiates lustful feuds among white suitors and the conflict of nature versus society in a manner almost identical to the author's non-white heroines in his racial fiction.

Chesnutt seems to draw further comparisons between Evelyn and his mulatta characters by suggesting that Evelyn herself may have African blood through her southern European ancestry. He would have certainly been aware of cultural and physiological similarities between ancient southern European and North African civilizations, particularly the Egyptians, even if theories of human migration out of Africa had not yet been formulated. More concrete textual evidence, however, points to the suggestion of Evelyn's African heritage. Chesnutt's use of the name "Evelyn" (onomastically derivative of "Eve"), for example, can be seen as an attempt to signify on what J. Lee Greene calls "the image of America as the new Eden" that permeates descriptions of the New World, first by European explorers and later by Protestants who justified slavery by asserting "that blacks were not descendents of the original parents and that their presence in the biblical Garden of Eden stemmed from the intruding evil (the snake)" (12–14). Greene argues that African American writers created their own version of the Eden narrative to combat Negrophobic representations of black relations with whites in the postbellum South: "these authors appropriate the character prototype and inscribe it as black female subjectivity, emphasizing physiological, sociological, psychological, and intellectual similarities between the novels' black heroines and southern white belles. It is a strategy designed to nullify Negrophobes' assertion that innate differences between blacks and whites justify blacks' continued marginal status in society" (48). Is it possible that Evelyn is part of this effort to combat white Negrophobia? Could she also be used by Chesnutt to introduce black ancestry into the mythical white Eden? Evelyn has some advantages in this tradition over Chesnutt's mulatta characters. As we have seen, her physiological features suggest non-white ancestry. However, she is also identified by other characters as white—taking on all the social, psychological, and intellectual features of a white belle. While she's not southern, the northern setting would presumably be more realistic for someone with "dark" physiological features to be unquestioningly considered white; thus, the reality of black ancestry is quietly infused into the white monolith. Knowing that his readership would never accept an identifiable "black" woman as a heroine, Evelyn might be Chesnutt's way of conceding to white readers' sensibilities while, at the same time, keeping Africans in the Eden of the New World without whites' knowledge.

Current literary and scientific research supports the view that Evelyn represents African ancestry among whites, and even goes to some length to suggest that Chesnutt's arguments on mixed-race ancestry and the effects of amalgamation are more accurate than Professor Ripley's. In *Chesnutt and the Fictions of Race*, Dean McWilliams explains that while "Ripley focuses on Europe, he does not directly address the American situation" that so preoccupied Chesnutt (51). McWilliams also recognizes that Ripley argues against racial intermingling, citing his assumptions that "mulattoes in any climate lack vitality; and unless a continual supply of white blood is kept up, they tend to degenerate" (qtd. in McWilliams 51). This passage marks the key theoretical difference between Ripley and Chesnutt, who, in contrast to Ripley, believed that humanity would benefit from racial amalgamation. Indeed, Chesnutt himself argues from his own "observation" and experience that "in a majority of cases people of mixed blood are very prolific and very long-lived" (Ferguson, "Future" 97). According to McWilliams, "modern scientific opinion supports Chesnutt on all major points," even though "the formation of that opinion and its full acceptance was, in 1900, still several decades in the future" (51). Indeed, Chesnutt did not have adequate scientific and anthropological evidence to prove his theories on racial amalgamation, and, even if he did, it would have certainly been met with brazen resistance by the prevailing racist ideology based on nineteenth-century pseudoscience and the emerging eugenics movement. And yet Chesnutt also seems prophetically conscious of a shared human ancestry that has been corroborated only in recent decades by genetic research.[13] In his essay "Race Prejudice," Chesnutt describes how laws and a legacy of racial segregation have interfered with his vision of racial amalgamation, arguing that "mixed blood," even "if it has not brought the Negro materially nearer to the white in color," has brought African Americans "farther from the ancestral type" (*Essays* 220). While Chesnutt clearly privileges the acquisition of fair skin as the means through which the race problem will be resolved, he also recognizes the "Negro" as the "ancestral type," suggesting that Chesnutt believed that an infusion of ancestral African blood, an inevitable aspect of the future American, has also already been occurring throughout human history.

If the description of Evelyn Thayer in the first museum scene exposes the myth of white racial purity and the historic instability of white identity, Chesnutt advances his argument in the second museum scene by specifically contrasting the earlier description of Evelyn's southern European ancestry to a racially ambiguous Greek immigrant. Again, Chesnutt seems to blame whites' "obliviousness to certain facts of human nature and human history" for creating arbitrary racial distinctions (Ferguson, "Future" 96). The Greek immigrant, for example, descends from the same people as Evelyn Thayer (implicitly) and the "colored" Venus (explicitly), but while they are seen as white, the immigrant's racial status is dubious. As Manson and Evelyn leave the museum, the narrator describes him as

a young Greek of the degenerate modern type which seeks our shores, to black our shoes, [who] stood in rapt devotion before a cast of the Discobolus. Somewhere in that insignificant head with its commonplace contour lurked some far-drawn ancestral love of beauty. The race had lost the imagination to conceive, the power to execute, but still retained, in the bootblack of the street, enough of the divine spark dimly to appreciate the work of its ancient forbears. (55)

Like the Discobolus, which itself is a degenerate copy of its Greek ancestor,[14] this "modern" immigrant occupies a depraved status in the United States. Unassimilated into the white mainstream, he is reduced to the menial work of shining shoes. The Greek man also has an "insignificant head" that seems to mock nineteenth-century pseudoscientific arguments that used head shape and size to argue for the racial "inferiority" of non-whites. Even though the Greek man presumably is more connected to his ancestry than the historically amnesiac white American citizen, his dim appreciation of the Discobolus replica seems to comment on whites' imagining that the "degenerate" state of the immigrant is somehow the result of poor breeding.

The Greek man thus complicates Chesnutt's use of art to interrogate whiteness: whereas Evelyn's "dark beauty" is compared to Venus and draws special attention from her white courtiers, the Greek, although from the same ancestry as Evelyn, is marked as non-white by his immigrant status and his social class. In fact, the question of class, in addition to ethnicity, was another discriminatory tool that whites used to decide whom they would assimilate. Immigrant groups such as the Irish, as noted above, were often considered racially different not only because of physiological differences or religious prejudice against Catholicism in a predominantly Protestant country, but also because they often did the same hard labor that was available to African Americans at the time. The Greek admirer of the Discobolus, as a shoe-shiner, seems no exception.

Manson, however, also needs to justify his whiteness in the face of caste prejudice, particularly since he is a product of the South, where the residue of an aristocratic caste system still held significant influence. This question of class bears on the novel's depiction of whiteness by exposing the dubious relationship between race and class in his family background. As Manson unveils his family history as mountain dwellers in Kentucky, he explains: "My people were not the descendants of cavaliers, proud of the deeds of their ancestors—not all of them noble— nor slave-holders drawing their wealth from the toil of other men. They were poor-whites—how poor you could hardly understand!" (49). Tracing the history of "white trash" in the United States, Matt Wray argues in *Not Quite White* that poor whites have a history of marginal racial status based on their socioeconomic conditions and that prejudice against poor whites and the emergence of the eugenics movement led to "involuntary institutionalization and sterilization of the poor and indigent" who were considered too degenerate to propagate the white race (19).[15] Continuing his family history, Manson explains how his "ignorant" ancestors had "no pride of race" because they had "no negroes [*sic*] among them, by comparison with whose estate to magnify their own" (50). Geographically and culturally isolated, Manson's Kentucky community had no basis on which to establish racial hierarchies: "all were poor and therefore all were equal" (51). Their shared poverty, and not their shared whiteness, is the determinant for equality. In the eyes of mainstream white America, however, they are a racially marginalized group: white in appearance, but socially ostracized by mainstream whites.

Chesnutt also wrote about the courtship of two poor white lovers, Ben Dudley and Graciella Treadwell, in *The Colonel's Dream*,[16] further illustrating his understanding of the way social class impacts the dubious category of white identity. Both the descendents of degenerating aristocratic families, the characters acquiesce to the possibility of a meager subsistence, but they squabble momentarily over the racial implications of their class status. When Graciella accepts that she will marry Ben and "be, all my life, a poor man's wife—a poor white man's wife," Ben responds: "No, Graciella, we might be poor, but not poor-white! Our blood will still be of the best" (274). Ben clearly differentiates here between a "poor" white and a "poor-white"; as long as he keeps the racial categorization out of this economic assessment, he preserves the possibility for socioeconomic mobility. In other words, he understands himself as a white (aristocratic) man who has limited resources, not a "poor-white," or those listless poor-whites contrasted throughout the novel with the poor—but more industrious—blacks. Graciella, however, reads the relationship between race and class in a way quite different from Ben, claiming, "It will be all the same. Blood without money may count for one generation, but it won't hold for two" (274). For Graciella, within two generations poverty will transform their white status (whose economic success and Anglo-Saxon heredity is assumed), to the socially non-white category of poor-white, who, despite all the advantages accorded to people with fair complexions, are too ill-bred (i.e., racially impure, according to aristocratic society) to be categorized simply as white.[17] Manson's family would have been subject to this same marginalization as their poverty and lack of "pride in race" gives them no framework on which to construct a white identity.

Chesnutt further distinguishes between Manson's poor white family and mainstream Southern whites by invoking the language of bondage and freedom, suggesting that they, like African Americans, were also the victims of an unjust and oppressive caste system. In Manson's view,

[his] people were emancipated by the Civil War—though they did not know it—no more than they had known they were slaves to ignorance and to a false social system. They fought for the Union by instinct, while the poor-whites of the valley fought, under a mistaken leadership, to perpetuate their own degradation. After the war, you good people of the North went South to teach the negroes [*sic*], who needed it badly enough, God knows; and after a while you discovered that there were neglected white people who might perchance be as well worth saving. (52)

Chesnutt clearly compares the conditions of the (stereotypical) poor white mountain folks with African Americans' enslavement. Both are depicted as the product of the unjust southern caste system, which is capable of manipulating people into perpetuating "their own degradation," either through consciously fighting for the "false social system" or by acquiescing to the identities and social roles imposed on them by white supremacists. Avoiding the simplistic equivocation of poor whites with African Americans, however, Chesnutt also notes important differences here: for a poor white like Manson, it is possible to reap the benefits of the Northern white liberal philanthropists who "went South" after the war to help in Reconstruction efforts, including educational programs. As Chesnutt makes clear through educated black characters like Tom Landry, in *Mandy Oxendine,* and the title character of *Paul Marchand, F.M.C.*, no amount of education can, in the United States, give black Americans a realistic opportunity to transgress the color line and to be accepted as equals to whites. As *The Colonel's Dream* indicates, good will and philanthropy likewise fail to provide social and economic opportunities for African Americans. In contrast, Manson, although clearly engaging in stereotypical and unrefined behavior that marks him as a poor-white, has education and a burgeoning reputation as a gifted architect; and by the end of the novel, that is enough to secure his whiteness. Thus, *contra* Matthew Wilson's claim that "Manson . . . insists on his people's investment in whiteness" (40), the exclusion of his poor white family from the white mainstream, coupled with his family's general isolation from racial points of comparison, proves that Manson moves *into* whiteness from a racially ambiguous position.

The novel's denouement in Brazil rounds off Chesnutt's argument about arbitrary racial distinctions, as he contrasts American notions of whiteness with the "curious experiments in ethnology and government" occurring in parts of South America at the time (*Evelyn's* 13). In her study of race and gender in Brazil, Elisa Larkin Nascimento argues that these experiments were, in fact, serving white supremacist agendas. While white supremacists in the United States reluctantly absorbed non-Anglo European immigrants into the white mainstream to maintain their majority, white supremacists in Brazil used tactics disturbingly reminiscent of Chesnutt's calls for racial amalgamation in the United States. Nascimento writes that "the solution [to the 'black stain' on Brazil's white population] was to create a new theory exalting race mixture by justifying it as a way to dilute the inferior African base of the Brazilian racial stock and strengthen the superior white component" (51). Under this logic, Brazil's white leadership would maintain white supremacy by eliminating "all vestiges of African descendents" through "mass European immigration" and "the subordination of [black] women," who, according to white supremacists, could not bear "racially pure" white children (51–52). With far different intentions and apparent ignorance of the white supremacist agenda in Brazil, Chesnutt praises their practice of amalgamation in the conclusion to *Evelyn's Husband* by describing the great extent to which it has been taking place in the city of Rio de Janeiro:

The population was typically South American; the people were of all shades, from the occasional German or English white, through the olive Latin of pure race to the stolid Indian or full-blood Negro, mixed breeds predominating, as though nature had selected this hot land as a laboratory for fusing again into one race the various types into which primeval man had in remote ages become differentiated. There was no great novelty in the scene to Cushing, to whom there were few strange scenes or peoples; and Manson's eyes were sealed. (253)

Whereas white Brazilians advocated this mixing as a means to maintain "supremacy," Chesnutt, always tacitly advocating for the whitening of American blacks through his exaltation of "predominantly white" amalgamated people like himself, also reminds his audience that white skin coloring, globally speaking, is a statistical and biological minority. In the above passage, for example, only an "occasional German or English white" exists in this microcosm of the world's diverse populations. While "there was no great novelty in the scene for Cushing," he nonetheless seeks out the American patient at the hospital (who turns out to be Evelyn's brother, Wentworth). As a white man abroad, Cushing is forced to recognize his own minority status and seeks out his own kind. As Chesnutt explains, "ties of race and country are always stronger in a foreign land. An American abroad will welcome a yellow dog from his native town" (*Evelyn's* 260). Racial distinctions are certainly important in Brazil, but they are made on completely different terms, to the point where a non-white "yellow dog," who would clearly be degraded by whites in the United States, in Brazil would appear as much of a countryman as any white person. Thus, in the context of a city which makes no qualms about its "racial-mixing," the distinctions between black and white, which so dominate the white American psyche, are of little relevance, ultimately exposing the arbitrariness of American racial designations.

The description of Rio de Janeiro also returns to the premise that humans share a common biological origin, as illustrated in the previous discussion of the biblical allusion to Eve and the suggestion that Evelyn is tied to a non-white ancestry. To allay any doubt about his stance on humanity's common origins, Chesnutt advances his argument for amalgamation in this description of Brazil by alluding to the "Future American" essays, where he says that the "curious experiments of ethnology and government," which promote (if not enforce) racial mixing, are a perfectly reasonable way to expedite the end of racism by eliminating all physiological markers of racial difference. For Chesnutt, Brazil is the "laboratory" where his theory can be tested, creating a homogenous humanity that resembles "primeval man." In his words, "all would be tarred with the same stick," and thus no one would care about the occasional African features of another (Ferguson, "Future" 99).[18] Unfortunately, Chesnutt's argument seems to backfire here as his views on Brazil, expressed so clearly in *Evelyn's Husband*, neglect the fact that white supremacists were using his "cure" for "race prejudice"[19] in the United States to advance their own racist agendas. Thus Chesnutt himself seems to have fallen victim to the slippery discourse of whiteness, which in Brazil has gone so far as to willingly infuse itself with all the world's blood and still call itself pure.

Given the diverse factors—such as physical appearance, social class, ethnic background, and the irrational fear of losing power—that contributed to the continual redefinition of whiteness during Chesnutt's career, how can one determine with any certainty what his white-life fiction accomplished? Furthermore, if critics refuse to take whiteness for granted and continue to expose it for what it is—a historically mutating racial construct used to advance the interests of white supremacists—then what else might we learn about whiteness through depictions of whites by African American authors? On one hand, *Evelyn's Husband*, as William L. Andrews states, was "a frankly commercial effort to appeal to the popular fancy" (131). In this way, Chesnutt merely followed his contemporary Paul Laurence Dunbar in trying to find literary success by writing white-life novels that used the conventions of romance, a wildly popular genre among whites in the 1890s.[20] There were, of course, some differences in what Chesnutt wanted to accomplish through the marked shifts in literary conventions and premises he used throughout his career, but these are not enough to sustain such arbitrary distinctions of genre.

I am reluctant to dismiss novels like *A Business Career* and *Evelyn's Husband* as merely unabashed efforts toward financial gain. Despite his commercial ambitions, Chesnutt, in the words of Ryan Simmons, always hints "at the racial ambiguity that potentially marks *any* individual's existence" (134). As such, critical approaches to Chesnutt's white-life fiction must look for these hints, interrogate them, and put them into the greater context of his life, time, and work. I have attempted to show through this approach that once whiteness is not taken for granted, it becomes possible to see how *Evelyn's Husband* participates in Chesnutt's critique of American racism by muddying up sharp racial categories, illusions of pure racial histories, and, ultimately, the arbitrary distinction between white-life and racial genres of fiction. The novel complicates and, in fact, challenges the distinction between white-life and racial fiction in that it represents whiteness itself as a slippery and historically shifting racial construction. As such, white-life fiction is simply not dialogically opposed to racial fiction. In the final analysis, white-life *is* racial fiction, participating in the same racial discourse that created the illusion of racial difference in the first place. Critical approaches to Chesnutt's work should avoid falling into the same discourse. After all, if we will truly honor Chesnutt's "universal subject position," we must begin by speaking and writing about his work in terms that acknowledge that Chesnutt wrote "as a human being… about other human beings" (*Essays* 514), *all* of whom were—and still are—bound to American racism.

Notes

1. Chesnutt Journal, April 23, 1879. This and all subsequent references to Chesnutt's journals are to *The Journals of Charles W. Chesnutt*, ed. Richard H. Brodhead.
2. Dividing Chesnutt's fiction into "racial" and "white-life" genres has a similar bifurcating effect and limits possibilities for critical analysis. For Wilson, "white-life" refers to works "that contain only incidental African-American characters and that concentrate on depictions of white experience" (xv), a seemingly benign definition that is nonetheless complicit with the idea of a uniform, non-racial "white experience" defined in opposition to "racial" identity.
3. *Evelyn's Husband* is one of three Chesnutt novels that deal almost exclusively with white characters. The other two are *A Business Career* (1898) and the unfinished manuscript "The Rainbow Chasers" (1900).
4. Matthew Wilson goes some distance to answer this question by turning to scholarly and historical accounts of how laws, heredity, and physiological markers were used both to define and to complicate white identity. Referring to the 1922 and 1923 Supreme Court cases on the issue, Wilson summarizes the decision saying that "if one is accepted, by common knowledge as white, one *is* white" (10). Indeed, this ruling is the moment when the bifurcation of white and black, heretofore defined (albeit inconsistently) by state-level courts, would become a uniform federal definition. *Evelyn's Husband* was written nearly two decades before this mandate, however, when who counted as "white" was still hotly contested on state and local levels.
5. The essay "What Is a White Man?" was originally published in *The Independent* on May 30, 1889. Chesnutt tentatively attributes this phrase to "Mr. Grady of Georgia," referring to Henry Woodfin Grady, a virulent advocate of the "New South," which would be understood in terms of Anglo-American domination.
6. The Thirteenth Amendment abolished slavery (1865); the Fourteenth Amendment granted due process and equal protection to all citizens (1868); the Fifteenth Amendment granted the right to vote to all citizens, regardless of "race," "color," or "previous condition of servitude" (1870).
7. The fear of "nigger domination" among Chesnutt's white characters is a prevalent theme in *The Marrow of Tradition*, where the organizers of the town riots constantly refer to their efforts in opposition to blacks gaining political and economic footing in the post-Reconstruction South. The novel is based on the race riots that occurred in Wilmington, NC, in 1898, where white supremacists raised mobs to kill and batter blacks to prevent their upward mobility.
8. Contemporary theories on globalization support Chesnutt's theory of white fear when confronted with the realities of black enfranchisement and millions of immigrants laying claim to American identities. In *Fear of Small Numbers*, Arjun Appadurai demonstrates how "majorities" historically demonstrate behavior that shows fear of the "risk of destruction by minorities, who know how to use the law (and the entire apparatus of liberal-democratic politics) to advance their special ends" (58). For Appadurai, the "logic of purity" of a majority leads to "rage about incomplete" purity that the majority (whites) exercise on the bodies of the perceived threat to purity (blacks and non-white European immigrants) (55).
9. A thorough investigation of this phenomenon as it pertains to the creation of an American ethnic group and its tension with a more liberal cosmopolitanism can be found in Eric P. Kaufmann's *The Rise and Fall of Anglo-America*. In regards to my discussion about Anglo-American fears of becoming a numerical minority in the United States, see Kaufmann's graph

of the percentage of the U.S. population from British Protestant descent, which was nearly 80 percent in 1790, dropping to a mere 55 percent by 1920 (27; Fig. 1).

10. Simmons's theoretical lens helps him expose this racial subtext: instead of distinguishing between Chesnutt's "white-life" novels and "racial fiction," Simmons splits Chesnutt's work between "Northern" and "Southern" fiction. While the Northern stories tend to focus on white characters, the geographic split makes more sense than the racial/nonracial distinction because it does not rely on the assumption of hardened racial categories, even if the Northern narratives tend to focus more on white characters.

11. The "Future American" essays were published in the *Boston Evening Transcript*: "What the Race Is Likely to Become in the Process of Time" on August 18, 1900, "A Stream of Dark Blood in the Veins of Southern Whites" on August 25, 1900, and "A Complete Race Amalgamation Likely to Occur" on September 1, 1900. SallyAnn H. Ferguson introduces and reprints these essays in *MELUS* 15.3 (1988): 95–107. All references to the "Future American" essays are to this reprinting.

12. The novella was rejected by Houghton Mifflin in 1897 for publication both as a book and as a serial piece in the *Atlantic*. It was finally edited by Charles Hackenberry (Urbana and Chicago: U of Illinois P, 1997).

13. Stephen Oppenheimer's authoritative book *The Real Eve: Modern Man's Journey out of Africa* documents the shared genetic make-up of humans that can be traced back to a "mitochondrial Eden" to approximately 190,000 years ago. According to Oppenheimer, non-African genetic mutations began to occur approximately 60,000 to 80,000 years ago (40, Fig. 0.3), corresponding to the first emigrations of humans from Africa, across the Arabian peninsula, and dispersing throughout the world.

14. The Discobolus of Myron is a marble reproduction of a lost bronze Greek statue. The mention of this statue, carved from white marble, might also be considered a comment on the tendency for modern whites to distort classical art to fit their own image. For historical documentation on the Discobolus, see J. J. Pollitt, *The Art of Ancient Greece: Documents and Sources*.

15. For a treatment of the eugenics movement in literature, see Lois A. Cuddy and Claire M. Roche's *Evolution and Eugenics in American Literature and Culture, 1880–1940*.

16. As mentioned in note 9, *The Colonel's Dream* occupies a liminal space in Wilson's schema of "white-life" and "racial fiction." In the chapter "The Eccentric Design of Charles W. Chesnutt's New South Novel," in *Whiteness in the Novels of Charles W. Chesnutt*, Wilson captures an excellent vision of the book as emblematic of Chesnutt's growing disillusionment at prospects for social change in the South, but he does not explain the novel's liminal status. Since the novel deals explicitly with race, however, it seems to fall into the racial fiction category, even though its cast of characters is generally white.

17. In *Engendering Whiteness*, Cecily Jones addresses the specific condition of poor white women in North Carolina. See especially chapter 2, entitled "'Worse than [white] men, much worse than the Negroes...': Sexuality, Labour and Poor White Women in North Carolina," and chapter 6, entitled "'She Would Labor Almost Night and Day': White Women, Property, Rights and Slaveholding in North Carolina."

18. Nearly two decades later, Chesnutt would experiment with this theory in *Paul Marchand, F.M.C.*, a novel in which a cadre of five "white," incredibly racist cousins would learn that one of them has African ancestry. None of them choose to identify who it is, and thus, according to the "Future American" theory, all would give up racist ideology. The novel concludes rather cynically, though, as four out of the five brothers become increasingly violent and try to maintain the fiction of racial purity by advocating for laws against black enfranchisement and miscegenation.

19. See Chesnutt's 1905 essay, "Race Prejudice: Its Causes and Its Cures," in *Essays* 214–237.

20. Dunbar expressed considerable frustration when white literary gatekeepers such as William Dean Howells sent black writers mixed messages, expecting them to write about blacks but

not to depict the harsh realities of black American experiences, nor to expect literary success reserved for their white contemporaries. For an analysis of Dunbar's literary reaction to such criticism, see Gene Jarrett's essay, "'We Must Write Like the White Men': Race, Realism, and Dunbar's Anomalous First Novel."

WORKS CITED

Andrews, William L. *The Literary Career of Charles W. Chesnutt*. Baton Rouge: Louisiana State UP, 1980.

Appadurai, Arjun. *Fear of Small Numbers*. Durham: Duke UP, 2006.

Brodhead, Richard H. *The Journals of Charles W. Chesnutt*. Durham: Duke UP, 1993.

Carter, Julian B. *The Heart of Whiteness: Normal Sexuality and Race in America, 1880–1940*. Durham: Duke UP, 2007.

Chesnutt, Charles W. *A Business Career*. Ed. Matthew Wilson and Marjan A. Van Schaik. Jackson: U of Mississippi P, 2005.

———. *Charles W. Chesnutt: Essays and Speeches*. Ed. Joseph R. McElrath Jr., Robert C. Leitz III, and Jesse S. Crisler. Stanford: Stanford UP, 1999.

———. *The Colonel's Dream*. Ed. SallyAnn H. Ferguson. New Milford, CT: Toby, 2004.

———. *Evelyn's Husband*. Ed. Matthew Wilson and Marjan A. Van Schaik. Jackson: U of Mississippi P, 2005.

———. *The House behind the Cedars*. Ed. William L. Andrews. Athens: U of Georgia P, 1988.

———. *The Journals of Charles W. Chesnutt*. Ed. Richard H. Brodhead. Durham: Duke UP, 1993.

———. *The Marrow of Tradition*. Boston: Bedford, 2002.

———. *Paul Marchand, F.M.C.* Ed. Matthew Wilson. Jackson: U of Mississippi P, 1998.

Cuddy, Lois A., and Claire M. Roche. *Evolution and Eugenics in American Literature and Culture, 1880–1940*. Lewisburg, PA: Bucknell UP, 2003.

Ferguson, SallyAnn H. "Charles W. Chesnutt's 'Future American.'" *MELUS* 15.3 (1988): 95–107.

———. "Introduction: Charles W. Chesnutt: An American Signifier." *Charles W. Chesnutt: Selected Writings*. Ed. SallyAnn H. Ferguson. Boston: Houghton, 2001. 1–11.

Greene, J. Lee. *Blacks in Eden: The African American Novel's First Century*. Charlottesville: UP of Virginia, 1996.

Jarrett, Gene. "'We Must Write Like the White Men': Race, Realism, and Dunbar's Anomalous First Novel." *Novel: A Forum on Fiction* 37.3 (2004): 303–325.

Jones, Cecily. *Engendering Whiteness: White Women and Colonialism in Barbados and North Carolina, 1627–1865*. Manchester, UK: Manchester UP, 2007.

Kaufmann, Eric P. *The Rise and Fall of Anglo-America*. Cambridge: Harvard UP, 2004.

Kivisto, Peter. *Multiculturalism in a Global Society*. Malden: Blackwell, 2002.

McWilliams, Dean. *Charles W. Chesnutt and the Fictions of Race*. Athens: U of Georgia P, 2002.

Nascimento, Elisa Larkin. *The Sorcery of Color: Identity, Race, and Gender in Brazil*. Philadelphia: Temple UP, 2007.

Oppenheimer, Stephen. *The Real Eve: Modern Man's Journey out of Africa*. New York: Carroll and Graf, 2004.

Pollitt, J. J. *The Art of Ancient Greece: Documents and Sources*. 2nd ed. Cambridge, UK: Cambridge UP, 1990.

Simmons, Ryan. *Chesnutt and Realism: A Study of the Novels*. Tuscaloosa: U of Alabama P, 2006.

Wilson, Matthew. *Whiteness in the Novels of Charles W. Chesnutt*. Jackson: UP of Mississippi, 2004.

Wray, Matt. *Not Quite White: White Trash and the Boundaries of Whiteness*. Durham: Duke UP, 2006.

Contributors

MARGARET D. BAUER, author of *The Fiction of Ellen Gilchrist* (1999) and *William Faulkner's Legacy: "What Shadow, What Stain, What Mark"* (2005), is the Rives Chair of Southern Literature, editor of the *North Carolina Literary Review*, and Professor of English at East Carolina University. Her articles on Southern writers have been published in such venues as *Mississippi Quarterly* and *Southern Literary Journal*, and her monograph *Understanding Tim Gautreaux* is forthcoming from the University of South Carolina Press.

KEITH BYERMAN is Professor of English, Women's Studies, and African American Studies at Indiana State University. He is the author or editor of six books on African American literature and culture, including *Remembering the Past in Contemporary African American Fiction* (2005) and *Seizing the Work: History, Art, and Self in the Work of W.E.B. Du Bois* (1994). He serves as associate editor of *African American Review.*

MARTHA J. CUTTER is Associate Professor of English and African American Studies at the University of Connecticut and the editor of *MELUS: Multi-Ethnic Literature of the United States.* Her first book, *Unruly Tongue: Language and Identity in American Women's Writing*, won the 2001 Nancy Dasher Award from the College English Association. Her second book, *Lost and Found in Translation: Contemporary Ethnic American Writing and the Politics of Language Diversity*, was published in 2005. Her articles have appeared in *American Literature, African American Literature, Women's Studies, Callaloo, Arizona Quarterly, Legacy, Criticism,* and in the collections *Mixed Race Literature* (2002) and *Passing and the Fictions of Identity* (1996).

SALLYANN H. FERGUSON is Associate Professor of African American and American Literature at the University of North Carolina at Greensboro. Her latest publications include *Charles W. Chesnutt: Selected Writings* (2001), a reprint edition of Chesnutt's novel *The Colonel's Dream* (2004), and *Nineteenth-Century Black Women's Literary Emergence: Evolutionary Spirituality, Sexuality, and*

Identity (2008). She is also a past two-term president of MELUS (The Society for the Study of Multi-Ethnic Literature of the United States).

DONALD B. GIBSON, Emeritus Professor of English, Rutgers University, New Brunswick, NJ, is among those of an earlier generation responsible for establishing during the 1960s and '70s the study of African American Literature as a discipline within the traditional study of English and American Literature. The trajectory of his *Five Black Writers: Essays on Richard Wright, Ralph Ellison, Langston Hughes, James Baldwin, and LeRoi Jones* (1970) (among the earliest of such modern collections of literary criticism of black writers) finds a fitting culmination in this essay on Chesnutt, his final formal critical effort after his 2001 retirement.

SCOTT THOMAS GIBSON is a doctoral student at the University of North Carolina at Greensboro. His research interests include multiethnic American Literature, multicultural theory, and composition pedagogy. Particular interests include the intersection of "race," culture, and nationality in novels, theories of amalgamation and hybridity, and representations of whiteness in novels by authors of different ethnic backgrounds. Currently, he is investigating the projection of future American racial identities by twentieth-century American writers.

ERNESTINE PICKENS GLASS is Professor Emerita, Department of English, Clark Atlanta University. She is co-founder of the Charles Waddell Chesnutt Association and a recipient of the Sylvia Lyons Render Award for her contribution to Chesnutt scholarship. She is author of *Charles W. Chesnutt and the Progressive Movement* (1994) and editor of *Frederick Douglass by Charles W. Chesnutt: A Centenary Edition* (2001).

AARON RITZENBERG teaches writing and American literature in the English department at Yale University. His research explores the relationship between literature and social change. His recent publications include articles on Harriet Beecher Stowe, Sherwood Anderson, and Michael Chabon. He is currently working on a book, *The Sentimental Touch*, which investigates emotion in American literature during the rise of managerial capitalism.

WERNER SOLLORS teaches African American Studies, English, and Comparative Literature at Harvard University. He is the author of the books *Beyond Ethnicity* and *Neither Black nor White yet Both* and the essay "The Goopher in Charles Chesnutt's Conjure Tales: Superstition, Ethnicity, and Modern Metamorphoses." He also edited *Theories of Ethnicity: A Classical*

Reader (1996), *An Anthology of Interracial Literature: Black-White Contacts in the Old World and the New* (2003), and the Library of America edition of *Charles W. Chesnutt's Novels, Stories, and Essays.*

SUSAN PROTHRO WRIGHT, Associate Professor at Clark Atlanta University, has published articles on Chesnutt and other nineteenth-century American authors in venues such as *CLA Journal, Western American Literature, MELUS,* and *Southern Literary Journal* and in the collection *Scribbling Women and the Short Story Form: Approaches by American and British Women Writers* (2008). She is past president of the Charles Waddell Chesnutt Association and remains active in the organization.

Index